HITLER

Germany's Fate or Germany's Misfortune?

943-LAU

+ STL

PERSONALITIES *and* POWERS

HITLER

Germany's Fate or Germany's Misfortune?

JOHN LAVER

Hodder & Stoughton

A MEMBER OF THE HODDER HEADLINE GROUP

0003676219 0010

Acknowledgments

The publishers would like to thank the following for their permission to
reproduce illustrations in this volume;
Camera Press cover
Suddeutscher p. 4; p. 12; p. 24; p. 31; p. 35
AKG London p. 36
Ullstein p. 8
David Low in the *Evening Standard* and Clifford Barryman in the *Washington
Star* courtesy of the Centre for the Study of Cartoons and Caricature,
University of Kent, Canterbury, Kent p. 71; p. 83; p. 87; p. 92

Every effort has been made to trace and acknowledge ownership of
copyright. The publishers will be glad to make suitable arrangements with
any copyright holder whom it has not been possible to contact.

British Library Cataloguing in Publication Data
A catalogue entry for this title is available from the British Library.

ISBN 0 340 62084 6

First published 1995

Impression number	10	9	8	7	6	5	4	3	2	1
Year		1999		1998		1997		1996		1995

Typeset by Litho Link Ltd, Welshpool, Powys.
Printed in Great Britain for Hodder & Stoughton Educational, a division of
Hodder Headline Plc, 338 Euston Road, London NW1 3BH by
Redwood Books, Trowbridge, Wiltshire.

CONTENTS

PREFACE

This book considers the life, opinions and influence of Adolf Hitler. When I first studied the Third Reich in depth, as a university student, the emphasis was very much on the development of Nazism and the structures of the Nazi state. There was a deliberate attempt to avoid a preoccupation with personality. At the same time, of course, I was aware of the many books on the market which focused on the life and personality of Hitler. Some of these studies were scholarly, some were sensational, verging upon the lurid. All testified to the fascination of the man.

At one level this interest in Hitler is ironic, given the tendency of many commentators to dwell upon the banality and coarseness of most of Hitler's ideas. But the attraction of Hitler as a subject for biography is also obvious. How *could* such a man, with unpromising beginnings, emerge from his provincial obscurity to become leader and dictator of a foreign country, and for a short time threaten to dominate the world, even, in Churchill's phrase, 'to plunge it into a new Dark Age'?

This book cannot, and does not pretend to be, an analysis of Nazism or the Nazi state. Nor is it a study of the development of Nazism as a political philosophy in a German or European context. These are major areas of interest which deserve studies of their own. But equally, I believe that any study of twentieth-century history would be seriously remiss if it did not take into account the role of key personalities like Hitler. Therefore, there is a clear focus to this book. It is essentially biographical, but assumes at least a basic knowledge of modern German and European history. The framework is chronological, but when appropriate, the focus is upon interpretation and analysis as much as telling the story. I intended to give equal weight to Hitler's ideas and his actions, and I have tried to relate the two. I hope I have succeeded. I have examined what Hitler said about himself, what contemporaries said about him, and what historians have concluded about him. I have considered the conclusions of several historians, both German and non-Germans. Sometimes I have added my own opinions which, of course, are as open to challenge as those of other writers whom I may have questioned. The opportunity to disagree is one of the fascinations of studying history.

It is impossible in a short study to consider all aspects of Hitler's life in depth. I have tried to examine major areas of concern and controversy, but the balance reflects my own particular interests. To gain a fuller appreciation of the subject, I hope that readers will consult some of the texts listed in the bibliography.

As always, thanks are due to Tim and especially Julie Laver for her informed support during the writing of this book.

INTRODUCTION

More than 30 years have now passed since in 1914 I made my modest contribution as a volunteer in the First World War, which was forced upon the Reich.

In these three decades I have been actuated solely by love and loyalty to my people . . .

It is untrue that I, or anyone else in Germany, wanted the war in 1939. It was desired and instigated solely by those international statesmen who were either of Jewish descent or worked for Jewish interests . . .

I myself, as founder and creator of this movement, have preferred death to cowardly abdication or even capitulation . . . May it at some time in the future become part of the code of honour of the German officer . . . that the leaders should march ahead as shining examples faithfully fulfilling their duty unto death.

The words were among the last spoken by Adolf Hitler. They were dictated as his will and testament to his secretary, on 29 April 1945, shortly before his suicide in the Berlin bunker. The Red Army was closing in for the kill. This document was typical of many of Hitler's utterances. Even at this stage of his career, with Germany collapsing in the face of an Allied onslaught from all directions, there was no word of self-recrimination or apology. Only the usual mixture of propaganda, bombast and self-delusion. It was true that Hitler had made a contribution to the First World War in a modest if brave capacity, but only an ardent German Nationalist could have agreed that the war had been 'forced' upon Germany. As for the following three decades, Hitler was surely as much motivated by a desire for power as 'love and loyalty' for his people, or at least a section of it. There was the usual tirade against Jewish influences supposedly responsible for the Second World War. Finally, having idealised the concept of the leader marching to a glorious death at the head of his followers, Hitler then chose perhaps the easier way out, suicide. In short, Hitler remained to the end the master of propaganda, as he had demonstrated back in the early days of the Nazi movement when his political career had been in its infancy.

Perhaps the gap between the image and the reality is one reason why Hitler has exercised such a fascination on posterity. This plus the natural interest in the career of a man who could emerge from an unprepossessing background to become, alongside Stalin, one of the most feared and loved leaders of his day. There are other reasons for the interest in Hitler. He came close to establishing a vicious dictatorship over Europe. His ideology was brutal but dynamic. Power attracts and fascinates as well as frightens. He was a man who offered positive and direct solutions at a time of uncertainty and despair. There might be lessons for the future:

> If Hitler's success was due less to the popular upsurge of the German people but rather to the skill with which he was able to exploit the stupidity and weakness of his opponents, then these seem to be factors which are likely to recur in any future situation where one politician is cleverer than the others, and there is very little that can be done about it.
>
> (J. Joll, *The Conquest Of The Past*, in E. Robertson, *The Origins Of The Second World War*, Macmillan, 1971, pp. 71–2)

So there are historical and contemporary reasons for the interest in Hitler, but there are challenges, too. Probably more is known about Hitler's life, including his early years, than other contemporary leaders such as Mussolini, Lenin and Stalin. Hitler had as great an impact as any of them, and yet there remain great controversies about him, in particular his motives, his policies and his methods of rule. Was he consistent or was he an opportunist? Did he take the initiative or did he respond to events? Were Goebbels and Schacht correct when they ascribed Hitler's success to his ability to simplify complex problems and find direct and brutal solutions to them – although this was the man who, for example, tolerated Göring's mismanagement of the air force at a crucial time of the war, from a sense of political devotion? This was hardly a Machiavellian trait. Hitler was the leader who presided over the Holocaust, yet showed a reluctance to bomb London, and until 1944 was remarkably ineffectual in dealing with domestic opponents. According to the revisionist historian David Irving, this was because Hitler was the weakest leader Germany has known this century – a far cry from the popular image of the all-powerful and forbidding dictator. How can there be so many different interpretations about a man who left his thoughts to posterity and whose life has been chronicled in detail? Is it partly, as Irving says, that 'The biggest problem in dealing analytically with Hitler is the aversion to him as a person created by years of intense wartime propaganda and emotive postwar historiography'? (D. Irving, *Hitler's War*, Hodder and Stoughton, 1977.)

As time passes, we can attempt perhaps to be less emotive. Generations born after Hitler's death will have their own prejudices, but different in nature perhaps from those of people who lived through the years when Hitler's decisions could affect the fate of millions.

Hitler's shadow lay over Germany and indeed Europe long after his death. To some extent it still does, and certainly the name continues to evoke strong passions in some quarters. Therefore, there is a contemporary relevance to a study of Hitler's life and career, as well as an historical interest in analysing the life of a man who for a brief period made history as well as being part of it; and who is still a focus of fear, fascination, and even incredulity, years after his death in the Berlin bunker.

SEARCHING FOR A ROLE, 1889–1914

ANCESTRY AND RACIAL PURITY

For a man whose career has exercised the pens of so many historians and biographers, the details of Hitler's ancestry are surprisingly hazy. This is principally due to the complexity of family relationships in the region of rural Austria which was Hitler's home. Inbreeding was a common characteristic. Hitler's father, Alois, was born to a domestic servant, Maria Ann Schickelgruber. She married a mill worker, but it was the latter's farmer brother, Johann Hiedler, who brought up Alois. In 1876 the 39-year-old Alois had his name officially changed, and misspelled in the process, to 'Hitler'.

Much later, rumours were spread that Alois's natural father had been Jewish. Adolf Hitler was concerned enough about the rumours to order an investigation into his forbears. His grandfather was shown to have worked in Graz for a Jewish family, which supported young Alois. Hitler denied that his grandfather could have been Jewish, and there is no convincing evidence that he was, but Hitler's lifelong obsession with his genealogy and 'purity of the blood' suggests some apprehension. However, it is not true, as has been claimed, that in 1938 Hitler ordered the destruction of the village in which his father had been born and his grandmother buried. He *did* lie about the birthplace of his ancestors, but then he lied about many things. It is difficult to construct a case that Hitler's own background explains the racist nature of the Third Reich. There were, after all, other Nazis who had no doubts about the purity of their own lineage and who were, nevertheless, fanatical about pursuing racist policies.

PARENTS

Despite his unpromising beginnings, Alois Hitler managed to carve out a career in the prestigious Austrian civil service. He was a customs official, with a reputation as a conscientious servant of the State. His personal life was less conventional. After two marriages and several liaisons, the 48-year-old Alois married his 25-year-old niece Klara Pölzl in 1885. Alois was domineering and often bullying at home. In contrast, Klara was a submissive, enduring wife, a devout Catholic. She suffered the loss of several children and stepchildren. Alois himself died in 1903, Klara in 1907.

CHILDHOOD

Adolf was born in April 1889, in an inn in the village of Braunau. The central Europe of Hitler's infancy was very different from that of today. Austria was the kernel of the Hapsburg or Austro-Hungarian Empire. The once magnificent Empire had survived revolutions in 1848, but after the Austro–Prussian War of 1866, Austria had been forced to abandon her pretensions to leadership of the German states, and the Empire had been transformed into the Dual Monarchy. After the First World War, the Empire was to be carved up and to lose territory to new states like Czechoslovakia and Yugoslavia. But at the time of Hitler's birth the Empire still presented a façade of stability. This was particularly true of the quiet rural area inhabited by Hitler's family.

There are no detailed accounts of Hitler's early years, and Hitler's own later writings display a tendency to exaggerate and dramatise. For example, his material circumstances were far more comfortable than he later maintained, given what we know about his parents' salary and pension. Nevertheless, we could not describe Hitler's childhood as happy. He was totally devoted to his mother, obsessively so. This was partly in reaction to his staid, bourgeois, domineering father. Alois Hitler was certainly not a sympathetic individual, and he has not had a good press from Hitler's biographers, but he perhaps had good reason to be unhappy with young Adolf's progress after promising beginnings in junior school. The family changed home frequently, and Hitler had attended five different schools before he was fifteen.

Reams have been written about Hitler's psychological state stemming from problems in the relationship between his parents, and how these problems manifested themselves throughout his later career. Hitler's mother was very protective towards him. Adolf liked to present himself as an 'artist' in perpetual conflict with his bullying father. Certainly such a childhood could influence some individuals into aggressive behaviour as a compensation for their own feelings of inadequacy or guilt – did Hitler regret that he had not protected his mother better? This may be partly the reason for Hitler's vindictiveness towards opponents in his later political life. However, without delving too deeply into psychoanalytical speculation about Hitler's state of mind, it is possible to identify certain traits evident in his personality from early childhood.

One trait was Hitler's obsessive need to talk, whether to a small or large audience. A close associate from his youth wrote:

> Soon I came to understand that our friendship endured largely for the reason that I was a patient listener . . . He just *had to talk* and needed somebody who would listen to him. I was often startled when he would make a speech to me, accompanied by vivid gestures, for my benefit alone . . . These speeches, usually delivered somewhere in the open, seemed to be like a volcano erupting.
>
> (A. Kubizek, *Young Hitler*, 1954)

These speeches were often accompanied by a quick temper. Hitler's other youthful characteristics were a liking for war games and a need to be the ringleader in activities with his contemporaries.

SCHOOL

Hitler's record in junior schools between the ages of six and eleven was exemplary. One teacher described him as 'mentally very much alert, obedient but lively.' At nine-years-old he was singing in a Benedictine abbey choir near Linz, and was thinking about a career as an abbot.

Upon entering the 'Realschule' in Linz in 1900 there was a dramatic change. Hitler was obliged to repeat one year and change schools. His grades were unsatisfactory in most subjects, and were particularly poor in German and Mathematics. Hitler's youthful letters display an appallingly low standard of spelling, grammar and handwriting, and

3

Hitler (X) at his primary school

overall a very weak command of written German – perhaps accounting for his preference for, and mastery of, the spoken word. Despite Hitler's later boasts of his prowess at History and Geography, his school record shows that he performed poorly in these subjects also.

Hitler's entire school career amounted to ten years, of which the last four were a struggle. He finally left to avoid repeating yet another year. It is not clear whether attitude or academic inability was the root cause of Hitler's difficulties. Probably it was his stubborn refusal to attempt anything in which he was not immediately interested. He claimed in 1942 that it was his teacher who had been at fault: 'Our teachers were absolute tyrants. They had no sympathy with youth; their one object was to stuff our brains and to turn us into erudite apes like themselves. If any pupil showed the slightest trace of originality, they persecuted him relentlessly.' He described most of his teachers as being 'slightly mad' and 'abnormal'. He also condemned them for personal 'uncleanliness' and 'presumptuous arrogance'.

In their turn, Hitler's teachers and school associates from his adolescent days recalled his argumentative nature, his extreme self-confidence, and his 'oddness'. Hitler's arrogance may have derived from family circumstances. He was disturbed at the age of 11 by the death of his younger brother Edmund, the more so when his anti-clerical father refused to attend the funeral and forbade his devout wife to do so also. The fact that several of his brothers and sisters had already died may have convinced both Hitler and his mother that he himself had been marked out by Destiny to survive for a special future.

A LIFE OF LEISURE IN LINZ

Hitler grew much happier after his father's death in 1903, although his friend Kubizek recalled that Adolf grieved at the time. August Kubizek, nine months Hitler's senior, was his only friend and his companion on frequent excursions. It was a friendship in which Hitler was very dominant. Although he enjoyed Kubizek's companionship, it was based upon the understanding that Kubizek rarely had the temerity to challenge Hitler's opinions. Hitler was to break off the relationship in 1908 without any explanation.

Free from his father's repressiveness, Hitler lived a life of bohemian pleasure, at home with his mother in Linz. He avoided school through real or feigned illness: the evidence of contemporaries is contradictory, although Hitler's claim that he had developed a serious lung complaint was certainly untrue. He lazed away his time principally by painting and indulging his chief passion, making architectural plans for a new Linz. Yet despite the grandiose schemes he produced, he was often listless and found difficulty in concentrating. He roamed the city with Kubizek, attended the opera, and for the first time heard the music of his beloved Wagner. Hitler also read widely. His tastes included: the philosopher Nietzsche; Karl May, the writer of westerns; and authors on military history and German history and mythology. Hitler had a prodigious memory, although he claimed that he often read only the last chapter of books, and gave an impression of wider learning than, in fact, he possessed.

At Linz Hitler fell in love with a girl called Stephanie. He admired her as an ideal, from a distance, and although he wrote to her and about her, he never dared speak to her.

Hitler moved to Vienna in order to seek admission to the Academy of

Fine Arts. But he returned to Linz late in 1907 to be with his mother, who was dying of cancer, although Bullock claimed that he returned only after her death. It was a time of great personal stress for Hitler: some historians refer to it as one of the great 'identity crises' of his life.

FEARS AND PREJUDICES

When Hitler returned to Vienna, he became, according to his testimony in *Mein Kampf*, a 'fanatical anti-Semite'. He described this as 'the greatest change I was ever to experience'. He encountered Jews, often pedlars from Eastern Europe, dressed distinctively, and he read anti-Semitic pamphlets. Some writers have seen a connection between the development of Hitler's anti-Semitism and the fact that his dying mother had been tended by a Jewish doctor. Others have written of Hitler being cheated by Jewish traders. There may be a simpler, less psychological explanation. Anti-Semitism was already deeply rooted in Vienna. Hitler may have sought to find reasons for his own unhappiness and failings by projecting hostility on to an identifiable group which had suffered persecution throughout its history. Personal experience may simply have reinforced views which Hitler had already absorbed elsewhere.

It should be emphasised that the insular inhabitants of Hitler's homeland were suspicious not just of Jews, but of all 'outsiders'. The latter included Protestant Germans from the North. After all, the Empire was a hotch-potch of competing nationalities, each with its deeply entrenched and sometimes mutually exclusive customs and traditions. Many of Hitler's teachers and fellow students at the Linz Realschule had been strongly nationalistic. This was certainly true of Hitler's History teacher, Leopold Poetsch, the one teacher whom he admired. In Linz Hitler probably read the virulently anti-Semitic newspapers that were full of vicious propaganda of the type later popularised by the Nazi *Der Stürmer*. Some of these newspapers already made use of the swastika as a nationalist symbol, and wrote of 'one *Volk*' and 'one Reich'.

Hitler also claimed that his experiences in Linz and Vienna taught him the 'meaning of history'. Like many other Austrians conscious of confronting different national groups, this meant for Hitler the necessity to fight for a pure nation state.

DOWN AND OUT IN VIENNA?

Vienna might contain peoples who became abhorrent to Hitler, but as the hub of the Empire and a thriving, vibrant and cosmopolitan city, it also had an attraction for someone of Hitler's temperament and ambitions, despite Bullock's comment that the city would have appeared 'callous and unfriendly' to him. Hitler certainly preferred to live there, away from relatives who might ask awkward questions about how he was going to earn a living. According to Kubizek, Hitler was very unstable at this time:

> He would fly into a temper at the slightest thing . . . He was at odds with the world. Wherever he looked he saw injustice, hate, and enmity . . . Choking with his catalogue of hates he would pour his fury over everything, against mankind in general who did not understand him, who did not appreciate him and by whom he was persecuted.

Hitler later claimed he had been so poor in Vienna that he had been forced to take menial jobs 'to earn my bread as a common labourer'. In reality he did nothing initially. His father's inheritance, an inheritance from a great-aunt, and an orphan's pension, provided him with a monthly income larger than that of a teacher. He rented rooms with Kubizek, slept in the mornings, and in the afternoons read, wrote, or went to the theatre. The only irritant was that while Kubizek graduated from the Conservatory of Music, Hitler failed to gain admittance to the Vienna Academy of Fine Arts. This led to another personal crisis, stimulating feelings of inadequacy and injustice which Hitler strove later to cover with bombast.

Hitler's failure led him to adopt a restless existence. Between September 1908 and 1909 he changed his address several times. His inheritance was probably exhausted, because he ended up in a hostel for the homeless. It may have been then, at the end of 1909, that Hitler briefly performed the manual labour of which he later boasted. He raised some money by painting and selling postcards and pictures of buildings and monuments, and completing advertising illustrations for cosmetics, footwear and women's underwear. Stories about Hitler's supposed penury came chiefly from the memoirs of two contemporaries, Reinhold

A drawing by Hitler

Hanisch and Josef Greiner, who were subsequently proved to be unreliable witnesses.

On receiving money from an aunt, Hitler moved at the end of 1909 to a home for men, and stayed there until May 1913. In relatively comfortable surroundings, he painted watercolours and sold them.

MUNICH

In May 1913 Hitler left Vienna for the great Bavarian city of Munich. He later gave several explanations for the move, chief among which was his contempt for an Austrian state which harboured different races and frustrated his own artistic ambitions. Perhaps the cosmopolitanism of Vienna had become too much for Hitler. The expanding city displayed extremes of wealth and poverty. The largest party in the Austrian Parliament was the Marxist Social Democrats, who comprised Czechs, Italians, Poles and Ruthenians in addition to Germans. Worst of all, Jews were prominent at all levels of society, and Hitler was unable to accept that they could ever assimilate into German life. Munich would be less tainted by all these 'faults'.

However, there was a more pressing and prosaic personal motive for Hitler to cross the border. He had failed to register for military service between 1909 and 1912, as he was legally obliged to do. Probably fearful of arrest, he moved to Munich. The Austrian authorities eventually caught up with him. Hitler was summonsed to appear before them in Linz. He wrote a pleading letter excusing his avoidance of service on the grounds of poverty:

> I have no friend other than Sorrow and Want, no companion other than unappeasable hunger; I have never known the beautiful word *Youth* . . . Despite the greatest deprivation, often in the midst of a dubious environment, I have always kept my name respectable before the law and clean before my conscience up to the time of this unanswered military summons, which I never even knew about at the time.

Hitler was allowed to appear in Salzburg rather than Linz to explain himself. He defended himself with characteristic persuasiveness, convincing the authorities that he was unfit for military service, and was released scot-free to return to Munich.

In the remaining months of peace, Hitler maintained his carefree existence in Munich. He continued to sleep until noon, paint and sell the pictures, and visit art galleries. If there was a fly in the ointment, it was the fact that he had conspicuously failed to proceed far along the great path he was convinced that Destiny had mapped out for him. Life was easy, but empty.

THE CALL TO ARMS

The coming of war in August 1914 was a great catalyst in Hitler's life. Like millions of other young men in Europe, he welcomed the call to arms as an opportunity to defend his country, which he now clearly identified as Germany. Paradoxically, many Austrians were more fervently nationalistic in the cause of the German Reich than the Germans themselves. This was possibly a reflection of the fact that Austria had once been the leading force in the old German Federation, and because Austrians increasingly faced challenges to their supremacy from other national groups within the Empire, such as Italians and Czechs. Hitler actually claimed in *Mein Kampf* that the Hapsburg Empire deserved to break up, and that the Austrians could only be truly free if they became part of Germany again.

The war also promised to fulfil a personal need, giving Hitler a feeling of identity. In his eyes he could now become an integral and important part of an efficient military machine, which had a clear purpose – victory over the Triple Entente, which threatened Germany. There are no indications of any doubts. Years later, Hitler wrote:

> To me personally those hours appeared like a *deliverance* from the vexatious moods of my youth. I am not ashamed even today to say that, overwhelmed by impassioned enthusiasm, I had fallen on my knees and thanked Heaven out of my overflowing heart that it had been granted to me the good fortune of being allowed to live in these times.

A MAN OF DESTINY

How can the 25-year-old future leader of Germany be characterised on the eve of the great conflagration which was to engulf Europe, and in Germany, give Hitler the first opening for a political career? He was a man convinced of his own innate abilities and frustrated that they were not recognised by others. He had internal feelings of inadequacy which he denied to himself, and for which he compensated by railing at the world. He was a loner with no apparent need for friends. Most acquaintances regarded him as a crank. When he launched into a political diatribe, his listeners were unsure whether to take him seriously or not. Obstinacy, oversensitivity, ambition, self-confidence: these were words which often came to mind when they described Hitler – although they also reported that he could go out of his way to be pleasant on the few occasions when it suited him. More disturbing is the fact that Hitler was already revealing psychopathic tendencies, marked by a lack of self-control and inner turmoil. These aspects only became truly dangerous in subsequent years. First, there was to be the joy of bearing arms in the cause of a Greater Germany. This was Hitler's opportunity to begin fulfilling his Destiny – one of his favourite words.

timeline	1889	Hitler's birth
	1903	Death of Alois Hitler
	1906	Hitler's first visit to Vienna
	1907	Death of Hitler's mother
	1908	Hitler took up residence in Vienna
	1913	Hitler moved to Munich
	1914	Outbreak of First World War

Points to consider

1) **What political views had Hitler formed by 1914?**
2) **What influences had formed those views?**

WAR AND POLITICAL AWAKENING, 1918–24

BRAVERY IN THE TRENCHES

On 1 August 1914, Hitler was one of a large crowd gathered in Munich's Odeonplatz enthusiastically greeting the declaration of war by Germany. He immediately petitioned for permission to enlist in a Bavarian army unit, the 16th Reserve Infantry Regiment. After rudimentary training

Hitler (left) as a frontline soldier, France 1917

Hitler was sent to France, in October. He was soon in action against British troops, and already by December he had been awarded the coveted Iron Cross Second Class. The award, for bravery, was on the recommendation of his regimental commander. Hitler described it as 'the happiest day of my life'.

Being in the army gave Hitler the feeling that he was sharing in the exercise of power, something for which he craved. He also had a purpose. Hitler was prone to distortion and downright lies in his reminiscences, for example he exaggerated the number of casualties suffered by his Regiment. Nevertheless, many aspects of Hitler's war record were impressive. In a war notable for its horror and large number of casualties, Hitler was fortunate to survive, but he did not have an easy war. He was a regimental dispatch runner, carrying messages between regimental and company headquarters. He survived 30 major battles and numerous dangerous missions. There is ample testimony to Hitler's bravery and professionalism. Friedrich Petz, one of Hitler's commanders, wrote in 1922:

> Hitler . . . was mentally very much all there and physically fresh, alert and hardy. His pluck was exceptional, as was the reckless courage with which he tackled dangerous situations and the hazards of battle.

A colonel wrote in the same year, before Hitler had become a national figure:

> Hitler set a shining example to those around him. His pluck and his exemplary bearing throughout each battle exerted a powerful influence on his comrades and this, combined with his admirable unpretentiousness, earned him the respect of superiors and equals alike.

In November Hitler was promoted to corporal, a rank he never surpassed. Why did such a reliable and long-serving soldier fail to rise beyond this rank? The key to this mystery lies in the fact that for all his courage, he was still a loner, prone to alternately muse by himself and harangue fellow soldiers on political matters. On one occasion he warned a comrade who had befriended a French girl about the dangers of interracial liaisons. Some of Hitler's behaviour seemed distinctly odd, such as his reluctance to take leave and his readiness to volunteer for extra duty. While earning a kind of respect, they were not attributes to endear him to fellow soldiers, and he did not show the qualities of leadership which his commanders were seeking. Alternatively, Hitler may not have wanted promotion.

The last of several conspicuous acts of bravery by Hitler was his saving the life of a wounded company commander in July 1918. For this he was awarded the Iron Cross First Class. In future years, political opponents spread rumours that the award was undeserved. Hitler said little about the award, but this was probably due to the fact that the officer who signed the recommendation was Jewish.

Hitler was not a typical soldier, concerned only for his own survival. He was fighting for greater issues. In a letter to a Munich acquaintance, written in February 1915, he declared:

> We further hope that the sacrifice and agony we suffer daily in our hundreds of thousands, the stream of bloodshed day after day against an international world of enemies, will not merely destroy Germany's enemies abroad but also break out internationalism at home.

DEFEAT AND DESPAIR

Hitler certainly suffered for the cause. In 1916 he was wounded in the thigh and was invalided for five months. In October 1918 he was temporarily blinded during a mustard-gas attack. He was recuperating in a Pomeranian military hospital when he heard the dramatic news on 7 November that Bavaria had become a Republic and that the war was over. On 21 November he was discharged from hospital and reported to his unit in Munich.

The fears caused by his injury were less traumatic than Hitler's concern for his beloved Germany. He could not accept that Germany had been beaten by superior military forces, nor that she had been beaten fairly. He was also horrified by news of revolution in Germany and the activities of Social Democrats and Communists there.

Hitler had to rationalise Germany's defeat. Part of the explanation, he was convinced, was that Kaiser Wilhelm II had allowed himself to be deceived and dominated by Jews and Marxists, two enemies which at this time were synonymous in Hitler's mind.

In what ways were Hitler's experiences in the First World War important to his future career? Surviving four years of war must have given him an insight into the psychology of soldiering and the minutiae of military life. This should have stood Hitler in good stead when he was commanding the Wehrmacht in the Second World War, but it could prove a hindrance. For example, he often condemned German soldiers to destruction by his refusal to permit a withdrawal in dangerous circumstances. This obstinacy had its roots in his experiences in the trenches in 1917 and 1918, when it was proved that infantry which held on to difficult positions frequently suffered fewer casualties in the long term than units which were ordered to retreat to other positions across open country. But until the war moved inexorably against Germany from 1942–3, Hitler often displayed as much acumen in military matters as his more experienced and better-trained generals.

Hitler claimed to have learned the importance of propaganda as a weapon in warfare from his experiences in 1914–18. The organisation of the Nazi Party was considerably influenced by the disciplined, male-orientated structure of the German army. The war did not inspire Hitler with the horror which was the abiding experience of many frontline veterans. This was because Hitler was already imbued with the Social Darwinist notion that war was natural to humanity, and that war between nation states was a purifying and uplifting force. As a participant in that process, Hitler felt that he was fulfilling the highest vocation open to man. This explains also why Hitler had been able to ignore the omens of defeat and remain optimistic right up to the Armistice. The end was all the more bitter when it came. However, that bitterness resolved itself into what Hitler was to call 'the most decisive decision of my life'. He decided to enter politics and restore Germany to its former greatness, and beyond.

WAR ON THE STREETS

Hitler returned to Munich at an inauspicious time for a German Nationalist. The collapse of the Imperial Government cleared the way for the politics of the street. Idealists and rabble-rousing demagogues established shortlived regimes, often created and crushed by violent means. The extreme left was responsible for establishing Soviet republics in several German cities, including Munich. Political murders were commonplace.

Hitler preferred the security of a continued army existence to the uncertainties of civilian life. He volunteered as a guard of Russian and French prisoners-of-war. He also read all the political literature available. He must have been fully aware of the violence and instability around him. Bavaria experienced more than any other state the activities not only of the revolutionary left but of paramilitary groups on the right, dissatisfied with the political chaos. In February 1919, Kurt Eisner, leader of the Bavarian Revolution of 1918, was murdered. After a period of Social Democratic government, a Soviet republic was proclaimed in Munich in April. It was overthrown by the army and Freikorps, bands of freebooting ex-servicemen. It was not simply a question of a right-wing backlash against the left. The situation was complicated by the historic antipathy in Catholic Bavaria towards Prussia and Northern Germany, and a correspondingly strong desire for separation or autonomy. Expression was given to this urge in March 1919 when a right-wing *putsch* or coup in Bavaria led to the establishment of a rightist government at odds with the central Berlin Government. A Republic had been proclaimed in Weimar. Bavaria was very much a refuge for those on the right who rejected the notion of parliamentary democracy, associated in their minds with defeat and the signing of the humiliating Treaty of Versailles. These Nationalists were quite prepared to murder 'traitors' like Erzberger, a signatory of the Treaty, if it furthered their hopes of replacing the Republic with a right-wing Nationalist regime, reinforced by a strong army. This in turn would restore Germany to her pre-war strength and dominance in Europe.

UNDERCOVER WORK

Hitler witnessed these dramatic events in 1919 and 1920. He was a member of an army that, deprived of allegiance to the Kaiser by the latter's abdication, operated almost as an autonomous force within the new State. Hitler avoided direct but dangerous political involvement until after the overthrow of the left, when he was given the task of tracking down soldiers who had supported the Soviets during their rule. They were duly executed. Hitler joined the Political Department of the army's VII District Command. As an 'Instruction Officer' his new role was to 'educate' soldiers against left-wing, pacifist or democratic ideas. While attending courses designed to combat Bolshevik ideas, courses which were financed by the Reichswehr (army) and private individuals, Hitler met likeminded colleagues for the first time.

Hitler attracted favourable notices from the military authorities for his skill in carrying out his duties. One report declared him to be 'an outstanding and fiery speaker, able to grip the attention of his listeners'. Hitler was certainly convinced that he had found a worthy role. In 1942 he recalled this period in Munich:

> When in 1918 the flags were lowered, my faith raised its head. But not my faith alone. My defiance too, rose against the idea of capitulation to a seemingly inevitable fate ... I at once resumed the struggle which tallied wholly with my conviction that only an internal struggle within our people could ensure the victorious emergence of the movement which would ultimately restore the German people in the eyes of other countries.

Hitler's ambition was less clearly defined in 1919 than he indicated in this reminiscence. But the situation was certainly favourable for him to begin to make some sort of mark. In *Mein Kampf*, Hitler wrote of overcoming great odds in the early days of his political career. In reality, the chaos of postwar Bavaria was an ideal breeding ground for the activities of someone with Hitler's sense of destiny and arrogance, plus a slice of luck when it mattered. Hitler's qualities may have been of marginal value in a stable society, but they exercised an appeal to many people who were inherently suspicious of the new democracy and free-for-all in Germany, and who were prepared to listen to inflammatory speeches against Jews, Socialists and other 'enemies' of 'true' Germans.

THE BEGINNINGS OF THE NAZI MOVEMENT
——

In September 1919 Hitler was ordered to investigate a small movement called the German Workers' Party. It had its origins in a group formed by a Munich locksmith, Anton Drexler. Drexler wished to appeal to the workers, but he was also a Nationalist who despised the internationalism and anti-militarism of the left. His party was formed in January 1919. Its 40 or so members met in Munich beerhalls to discuss politics. Hitler attended a meeting on 12 September 1919 and was moved to speak out strongly against proposals that Bavaria should secede from Germany and join Austria. Drexler was impressed enough by the outburst to send Hitler an invitation later to attend a committee meeting. Hitler did attend, without much enthusiasm at first, but soon agreed to join the party as its seventh committee member and fifty-fifth party member. Once again, this was to be classified as 'the most important decision' of Hitler's life.

There was an obvious attraction for Hitler in joining a small, obscure party in which there were no serious rivals to thwart his own grandiose ambitions. But at first progress was slow. Hitler made his first speech as a party member in October, to an audience of 111.

Early in 1920 Hitler was put in charge of propaganda. He now began to call himself 'writer' rather than 'artist'. He advertised a meeting for 24 February 1920. Almost 2,000 people attended. At this meeting Hitler announced the party's new name: the National Socialist German Workers' Party (NSDAP). A Twenty-Five Point Programme was also announced. The intention of the name was to differentiate the NSDAP from Socialist parties. Hitler was clearly the driving force in the party, and he left the army in April in order to devote all his energies to his new career.

THE QUALITIES OF LEADERSHIP

Hitler's oratorical skills were an important factor in winning support for the NSDAP. However, oratory alone does not make successful leaders. In Russia Trotsky was a greater orator than Lenin or Stalin, but he never achieved the eminence of either in the Communist Party. Hitler, despite the artistic temperament which had inclined him towards an easy-going existence before 1914, could also display considerable organisational skills when he put his mind to it. He had the toughness, the singleminded determination, and the support of Ernst Röhm. Already a member of the German Workers' Party, Röhm was, more importantly, a captain in the Munich Army District Command. Röhm's political views were similar to Hitler's. He was quite prepared to involve the army in politics. He helped to divert army funds into the new party, he recruited ex-soldiers into its ranks, and he helped to secure for Hitler the tolerance of the army, necessary given its powerful position in Bavaria.

Without this combination of Hitler's oratorical, propagandist and organisational skills, and help from likeminded colleagues, it is unlikely that Hitler could ever have raised the nascent Nazi movement above the other rival right-wing forces competing for support in the beerhalls and on the streets of Munich. Hitler's determination to bend the party to his own will inevitably provoked resentment and a backlash from some colleagues, who in 1921 even proposed an amalgamation with other nationalistic groups in order to restrict Hitler's power. Hitler felt strong enough and so secure in the knowledge of his importance to the party that he offered his resignation, sure of its refusal. Then he demanded further powers. Soon he was appointed the party's President. The party Committee then was soon dissolved, and Hitler ran the party dictatorially. Any member who tried to change the party programme would be expelled. Hitler knew he was indispensable. The party had already become his personal instrument. Hitler also secured control of other right-wing groups in and around Munich, and in Austria.

THE PROGRAMME

What features made the Nazi Party distinct in these early days? The Twenty-Five Point Programme adopted in February 1920 was drawn up by Hitler and others. It was nationalistic, demanding the abrogation of the Treaty of Versailles and the creation of a Greater Germany. It was anti-Semitic, demanding the exclusion of Jews from German society. It was anti-capitalist, calling for anti-monopolistic measures and the abolition of unearned income.

Most of these demands were not new, although the combination of Nationalist and Socialist measures was relatively unusual. The demand for a radical revision of the Treaty of Versailles did show Hitler's own influence. The programme may have won support among elements of the working and lower middle classes, but Hitler was not interested in the Twenty-Five Points as philosophical ideals or practical policies. Indeed, he was prepared to offer any programme to win support for his movement, and likewise, he was prepared to welcome support from any quarter. There are many politicians for whom political programmes are only means to an end, but Hitler was one of a new breed of politician – Mussolini was another – for whom power was a goal in itself. Any promises or slogans were legitimate tactics in the struggle to achieve power.

Although Hitler may have seen the programme only as a means of gaining a mass following, it won him notice in other right-wing circles, some quite influential. The process began whereby people who regarded themselves as Hitler's intellectual and social superiors believed that they could use his support while 'taming' him. This was a fatal delusion which was to culminate in the disastrous mistake of January 1933 when Hitler was appointed Chancellor.

PROPAGANDA

The nature and use of propaganda by Hitler was another remarkable feature of his movement. Hitler's mastery of the techniques of propaganda was one of the major reasons for the early successes of Nazism. The passages on propaganda in *Mein Kampf* were to be some of the most illuminating in the book. The political condition of Germany in the early 1920s made many Germans susceptible to propaganda, but Hitler showed great skill in exploiting the situation. He was adept at presenting slogans as facts: thus his statement that propaganda was 'a means and must be judged with regard to its end'. All propaganda must be based on the supposition that the masses, whom Hitler despised, were not interested in logic or truth. The people needed certainties, or slogans dressed up as certainties. These slogans must be kept simple, because the masses had poor memories. Propaganda should express the same message over and over again and be aimed at the lowest common denominator. Truth was immaterial. In fact the bigger the lie, the better:

> The great masses of people . . . will more easily fall victim to a great lie than to a small one, since they themselves . . . lie sometimes in little things . . . Thus such an untruth will not at all enter their heads . . . therefore, just for this reason, some part of the most impudent lie will remain and stick.
>
> (*Mein Kampf*)

Hitler declared that crowds were 'feminine' by nature and therefore susceptible to emotional persuasion rather than logic.

Emotional persuasion was frequently achieved through the use of striking colours, flags, lighting and other tricks to enhance the effects of Hitler's public appearances and speechmaking. The meeting was to play an important part in Hitler's political armoury.

THE ORATOR

I have already referred to Hitler's power of oratory. He put great faith in the spoken word, more so than in the written word. This is not surprising given Hitler's skill at public speaking. It is not easy to appreciate this fact, since film extracts often show him at the climax of a long speech when he and his audience were seemingly in a state of near-hysteria. These extracts do not show the long and gradual build-up. There was nothing accidental about the process: the speeches were carefully planned and rehearsed. Hitler made notes and also relied upon his prodigious memory to make speeches often of two hours in length, while retaining the impression of spontaneity. Hitler practised his gestures, studied photographs of himself in action, and studied oratorical techniques in detail. In the early days meetings were often stormy, and Hitler dealt expertly with hecklers. In later years the audiences were larger and contained only supporters, but the meetings were always carefully stage-managed pieces of theatre. Although the crowds at these meetings were whipped into an ecstasy of neo-religious intensity, Hitler himself retained his self-control, while giving the impression that he was carried away on the same tide of enthusiasm.

Hitler's effect on an audience could be electric, as a supporter remembered from 1926:

> A storm of jubilation rising from afar, from the street and moving into the lobby, announced the coming of the Führer. And then suddenly the auditorium went wild, as he strode resolutely in his raincoat and without a hat to the rostrum. When the speech came to an end, I could not see out of my eyes any more. There were tears in my eyes, my throat was all tight from crying. A liberating scream of the purest enthusiasm discharged the unbearable tension as the auditorium rocked

with applause. I looked round discreetly, and noticed that others, too, men and women and young fellows were as deeply affected as I ... There were people around me who felt the same as I, who were looking at each other in joyful rapture, as if they were all one family or a brotherhood or a new firm and happy community where everyone could read in the other's eyes a solemn oath of loyalty.

quoted in P. Merkl, *Political Violence Under the Swastika* (Princeton, 1975)

HITLER'S SUPPORTERS

Who were the supporters in the early days? There are relatively few reliable analyses of the nature of Nazi support in the early years. A German study from the early 1970s investigated the 1923 Party List of 4,800 members and discovered that 31 per cent were lower middle class in status, 13.6 per cent small businessmen and shopkeepers, 11.1 per cent clerks, 6.2 per cent minor officials, 25 per cent skilled working class, 9.5 per cent unskilled working class,. There was as yet little support for the Nazis in rural areas. However, given that these social classifications are very broad, and other parties also gained considerable support from these groups, it would be dangerous to draw too many firm conclusions about Hitler's appeal, at least until the Depression brought about a big upturn in support for the Nazis.

Having commented upon the power of Hitler's oratory, it must also be stated that there is a danger in overrating the impact of Hitler's personal magnetism as a factor in attracting party members. Peter Merkl's study showed that only a third of party members joined after attending a party meeting. However, it appears that many of the younger members who were either ex-soldiers or were too young to have fought in the war, were personally attracted to Hitler. It was these men who formed the backbone of the strongarm squads which made violence a distinctive feature of the new movement by 1922.

Some individuals who later became famous in their own right were comrades of Hitler from the early days. Ernst Röhm has already been mentioned. Rudolf Hess and Hermann Göring were two other ex-officers who admired Hitler. Alfred Rosenberg, with pretensions as the movement's chief philosopher, and the perverted journalist Julius

Streicher, were other early colleagues. Dietrich Eckart, son of a lawyer, was very influential. Although he died in 1923, his anti-Semitism had influenced Hitler and he was the first publisher of the Nazi newspaper *Völkischer Beobachter*. (Hitler later dictated *Mein Kampf* to Eckart.) Hitler accepted that many of his early followers were rough and unstable individuals, but at the time he needed such 'fine chaps':

> I specially looked for people of dishevelled appearance. A bourgeois in a stiff collar would have bitched up everything.
>
> (*Hitler's Table Talk*)

INTIMIDATION

A feature of Hitler's movement in its early days was its use of terror and violence as a political weapon. This was not, of course, an original tactic, but Hitler showed a keen understanding of the possibilities of both intimidating opponents and impressing ordinary Germans with the power of the Nazis. Hitler appreciated that violence can simultaneously attract and repel. He did not invent the phrase 'Defence is the best form of attack', but he did translate it into action. In 1920 squads of thugs first became active in the movement. In August 1921 they were organised into the 'Gymnastic and Sports Division', a necessary euphamism since the Freikorps and Defence Leagues had been banned. In October 1921 the new organisation became the *Sturmabteilung* (SA). Its brown-shirted members both protected Hitler's meetings and took the battle into the streets and meetings of political opponents like the Communists. In Hitler's famous declaration, 'the reputation of our hall-guard squads stamped us as a political fighting force and not as a debating society'.

As an individual, Hitler was obsessed with both creativity and destruction. He cultivated an image of brutality – a word which Hitler often used. He once declared: 'Why babble about brutality and be indignant about tortures? The masses want that. They need something that will give them a thrill of terror.' A psychologist's interpretation might be that Hitler saw brutality as a masculine trait and harped upon it to hide feelings of personal inadequacy. For Hitler, to surrender or show tenderness were 'feminine' qualities to be despised. However, there were political advantages to be gained in Weimar Germany from using force, without resorting to psychological interpretations. Hitler was not

Hitler in Nazi Party uniform

the first nor the last politician to discover the possibility of promoting violence and then claiming to be the one political leader capable of suppressing the disorder which the violence created.

THE 1923 PUTSCH

In September 1921 Hitler led his followers in breaking up a political meeting of the Bavarian League, which advocated a federal solution to Germany's problems. A new, more moderate Bavarian Government put Hitler into prison for one month for this offence, in the summer of 1922. Although the government was soon replaced by a more nationalist one, Hitler was soon embroiled in difficulties with the latter. In order to influence events in Germany as a whole, Hitler needed the support of the Bavarian authorities. However, these, while nationalistic in outlook, were divided among themselves about the way ahead. Some favoured an autonomous Bavaria, some union with Austria, some an attempt to replace the government in Berlin. The Bavarian authorities saw Hitler's potential as an agitator, but were concerned about the difficulty of controlling the Nazi movement.

Hitler's mounting frustration was exemplified by a speech in Munich in November 1922:

> The Marxists taught – If you will not be my brother, I will bash your skull in. Our motto shall be – If you will not be a German, I will bash your skull in. For we are convinced that we cannot succeed without a struggle. We have to fight with ideas, but, if necessary, also with our fists.

In 1923 Hitler sought to take advantage of Germany's economic plight by trying to unite Nationalist groups in Bavaria and then march on Berlin. This was shortly after Mussolini's 'March on Rome'. The cessation of German reparations to the Allies, the resulting French occupation of the Ruhr, and rampant inflation, all seemed to justify Hitler's denunciations of the Weimar regime. He attempted a Putsch, or forcible takeover of power, in Munich. An effort in May 1923 was exposed as a bluff: he was forced to abandon his plans in the face of army opposition. Yet a sympathetic judiciary ensured that no action was taken against Hitler, and he was encouraged by mounting economic and political difficulties to renew his attacks on the government.

This time Hitler had the support of the First World War commander Ludendorff, a national hero. When the Berlin Government called off a campaign of passive resistance in Bavaria, Hitler and other Nationalist colleagues decided to act. A meeting of leading Bavarian politicians was held in Munich on 8 November. Hitler was present, and when his brownshirts invaded the meeting, he proclaimed a 'National Revolution' and a coup. However, the army stood firm. When the Nazis marched on the Reichswehr Headquarters on the following day, the police opened fire. Sixteen Nazis were killed, and Hitler lost his nerve. In pain from a dislocated shoulder, sustained in being thrown to the ground during the drama, he was driven away. Two days later he was arrested.

Hitler's Putsch might be viewed as a gamble, but he was in a difficult political position. Having blustered and threatened action, he had to offer something to his expectant followers, who might otherwise desert him. On the other hand, there was the example of Mussolini. It is also likely that at this stage Hitler was not expecting that he himself would be the sole arbiter of a new Nationalist government, but just have a share in the power, and he may have hoped that the masses would be inspired by his example to force through a revolution. If this was the case, it was a miscalculation which could have ended Hitler's political career.

Hitler was certainly despondent. Before his arrest, he was reported as having threatened suicide. Contemporaries assumed that Hitler was finished, but with characteristic skill, he was to turn his trial for treason into a vindication of his career, and was to present himself as a martyr to German national pride.

PRINCIPLES AND PREJUDICES

Was Hitler simply an opportunist, bent on power, or did he have any principles or ideas sustaining his early political career? It would be simplistic to dismiss Hitler as a power-crazed cynic. During his life up to and including 1924, Hitler had absorbed a mish-mash of ideas from various sources, and they became part of his intellectual and emotional make-up. Already by the time of the First World War he had formed definite ideas on a number of issues. Many of these were simply prejudices or negative emotions: for example his hatred of democracy, of Jews, of trade unions. He had also read widely. His tastes ran to a range of novels, plays and poetry. Indeed, he had made his own amateurish efforts as a writer in these fields.

After the war Hitler's reading became more utilitarian. While still reading about art, architecture, history, music and medicine, he became increasingly interested in works which would inform his political ambition. Like many people, Hitler's reading mainly reinforced his own prejudices – he dogmatically rejected any opinions with which he was not in immediate sympathy. Yet he always displayed a remarkable capacity to debate in great detail subjects such as war and art with professionals in those fields. This was partly due to Hitler's prodigious memory. His understanding may not always have matched his knowledge, but nevertheless Hitler was able to impress intelligent observers with his apparent erudition.

Many of Hitler's ideas were absorbed from relatively obscure sources. These included many books and articles on race. Some of Hitler's ideas on propaganda were taken from Le Bon's *The Crowd, A Study Of The Popular Mind*, published in Vienna in 1912. Hitler's ideas on pan-Germanism and the inequality of human races were stimulated by works like Houston Stewart Chamberlain's *Foundations Of The Nineteenth Century* and Gobineau's *Essay On The Inequalities Of The Human Races*. Gobineau held the pessimistic view that the 'pure' races were doomed to be contaminated by mixing with inferior ones. But Chamberlain believed that the Aryan race, which he identified with Germany, had a great future if it avoided corrupt Jewish influences. Hitler became a firm disciple of this view.

Social Darwinism was a strong influence on Hitler. It was an adaptation of the theories of Charles Darwin. Its proponents accepted that all life was in essence a struggle for survival, and that only the strongest and fittest should survive. Social Darwinist ideas were widely discussed in Germany and other European countries in late nineteenth-century Europe, and it was natural that Hitler, a voracious reader, should have encountered them. The ideas later found their ultimate expression in the Third Reich's programme of deliberately promoting the 'superior' Aryan race at the expense of lesser beings. Social Darwinists like Hitler lacked sentimentality, because sentimentality was a wasted, unnatural emotion in a world subject to the harsh laws of nature.

ANTI-SEMITISM
—

The particular emphasis in Nazism on anti-Semitism did not derive just from the pseudo-scientific theories described above. Hitler had come across anti-Semitic prejudice in pre-war Vienna. He was probably influenced by the racist pamphlets and newspapers he read in Vienna, particularly those written by Georg von Liebenfels and Guido von List. These men wrote brief, mystical pamphlets on subjects like racial pollution. Hitler was also influenced by Theodor Fritsch, who wrote the influential *Handbook Of The Jewish Question*, arguing that the Jews were gradually taking control of the world. Hitler also shared the anti-Semitic prejudices of one of his heroes, the composer Wagner; and he was acquainted with the *Protocols Of The Elders of Zion*. After the war, Hitler's racial prejudices were confirmed by Dietrich Eckart.

Anti-Semitism revived in Germany after 1918, as economic problems mounted and many Jews migrated into Germany from Eastern Europe. Other right-wing groups besides the Nazis played the anti-Semitic card, the more so since there were many Jews, for example Trotsky and Eisner, prominent in the world Communist and Socialist movements.

Hitler may also have had more personal reasons for anti-Jewish prejudice. Psychoanalysts have related this possibility to his widely rumoured sexual perversion. However, it should be emphasised that after 1924 Hitler's anti-Semitism was to be far less prominent in his public speeches. Was this because material conditions were improving, and there was less use for a scapegoat? If so, it reinforces the argument that, whatever Hitler's personal beliefs, he adapted his message to the nature of the audience he was addressing. This was Hitler the consummate politician rather than Hitler the unbridled fanatic.

HITLER AND HISTORY
—

Hitler was obsessed with history, and about his own place in it. He was equally interested in mythology, and the frontiers between history and mythology were frequently blurred in his mind. He claimed to draw his own inspiration from the ancient world, and blamed Christianity among other things for the decline of ancient virtues. He was totally opposed to the Marxist analysis of history as a succession of class struggles. To Hitler, history was made by great men. He regarded religion as a social necessity, but he himself believed only in a vague form of 'Providence' which guided his actions. In 1942 he condemned Christianity as being inferior to most other beliefs:

> It's enough to make a sensible German tear his hair out to see Germans reduced by Jewish muck and priestly drivel to the sort of behaviour we find so ludicrous in negroes and howling Turkish dervishes. And what is particularly infuriating is that, while religious teaching in other parts of the world – that of Confucius, Buddha and Mohammed, for instance – has provided religious-minded people with a broad spiritual basis, Germans have been landed with theological expositions lacking all real depth.

Hitler of course was not unique in his prejudices. Unfortunately for the world, he was to attain a position from which he was able to translate some of his prejudices into reality, with devastating effect.

timeline	1918	End of First World War
	1919	Setting up of the Weimar Republic and signing of the Treaty of Versailles
		Hitler joined the German Workers' Party
	1920	Formation of National Socialist German Workers' Party
	1921	Formation of SA
	1923	November Putsch in Munich and Hitler's arrest

Points to consider

1) How significant was the First World War in Hitler's career?
2) What were the main features and beliefs of the Nazi Party in the years 1920–3?
3) From where did the Nazi Party get its support in the early years?
4) What were Hitler's views on propaganda?
5) What qualities did Hitler display as a party leader in the years before 1923?
6) What was the significance of the Munich Putsch?
7) What were Hitler's beliefs in the years up to 1923, and what were the influences upon them?

FROM PRISON TO THE CHANCELLERY, 1924–33

PRISON AND *MEIN KAMPF*
—

Hitler's trial for treason, following the failure of the November Putsch, began in Munich in February 1924. Far from being abashed, Hitler took the offensive during the trial. He dominated proceedings by taking responsibility for the attempted coup and continuing his attacks on the Weimar Republic. Sympathetic judges allowed him to make long and eloquent speeches:

> The army we have formed is growing from day to day ...
> I nourish the proud hope that one day the hour will come when
> these rough companies will grow to battalions, the battalions to
> regiments, the regiments to divisions, that the old cockade will
> be taken from the mud, that the old flags will wave again ... It
> is not you, gentlemen, who pass judgement on us. That
> judgement is spoken by the eternal court of history ... You
> may pronounce us guilty a thousand times over, but the
> goddess of the eternal court of history will smile and tear to
> tatters the brief of the State Prosecutor and the sentence of the
> court. For she acquits us.

It was inevitable that Hitler would be found guilty, but he was given the minimum sentence of five years.

The failure of the Putsch reinforced Hitler's conviction that violent revolution was an unproductive course. He would win power by legal

Hitler in Landsberg Prison

means, using the parliamentary mechanisms which he detested and would eventually destroy.

Hitler was in prison only from November 1923 to December 1924, when an amnesty ended his detention. The Landsberg prison fortress was comparatively comfortable, and Hitler received a stream of visitors, read, and dictated the first part of *Mein Kampf* to Hess, one of 40 other Nazis imprisoned there. Meanwhile the Nazi Party had been banned and was left as an ineffective rump, partly because Rosenberg, Hitler's choice as temporary leader, was incapable of asserting his authority – which was probably the reason why Hitler had chosen him in the first place. It suited Hitler for the party to remain weak and divided during his incarceration. While in prison himself, Hitler behaved as dictatorially towards fellow Nazis as ever.

Prison gave Hitler the opportunity to write a substantial book for the first time. Some of his colleagues had already produced their own efforts. *Mein Kampf* (My Struggle) was partly autobiographical, although it is often misleading as source material about Hitler's life. Much of the book

Franz Eher Nachf. G. m. b. H.

Deutschvölkische Verlagsbuchhandlung

Fernruf 20047 • München • Thierschstraße 15

Postscheck-Konto: Nr. 11340 München
Bank-Konto: Deutsche Hansabant A.-G. München

Kommissionär:
Herr Robert Hoffmann, Leipzig

4½ Jahre Kampf

gegen Lüge, Dummheit und Feigheit

Eine Abrechnung von Adolf Hitler

Leitspruch

„Sie müssen sich gegenseitig wieder achten lernen, der Arbeiter der Stirne den Arbeiter der Faust und umgekehrt. Keiner von beiden bestünde ohne den anderen. Aus ihnen heraus muß sich ein neuer Mensch kristallisieren: Der Mensch des kommenden Deutschen Reiches!"

Adolf Hitler.

Der Eher-Verlag kündigt „Mein Kampf" an. 1924

Die kürzere Fassung des endgültigen Titels ist wesentlich schlagkräftiger!

Hauptarchiv der NSDAP, München, Barer Straße 15

An advertisement for Mein Kampf *bearing its original title* is, however, an outpouring of Hitler's ideas. The first volume was dictated to Emil Maurice and Rudolf Hess, and Hitler read out selected passages to fellow Nazi prisoners.

Mein Kampf became one of the world's most published books. It also contained more than 164,000 errors of German grammar and syntax. The book simply confirms that Hitler was more comfortable with the spoken rather than the written word. An example of Hitler's tortured and muddled style is his reference to being strangled by 'Dame Poverty': 'Whoever has not himself been on the tentacles of this throttling viper will never know its fangs.' As a critic pointed out as early as 1936 (Rudolf Olden in *Hitler*), a viper does not have tentacles, a snake which kills with its coils has no venom, and a man being throttled by a snake would not feel its fangs. But *Mein Kampf* is above all a prime example of how Hitler managed to combine a half-baked ideology with occasionally perceptive ideas on propaganda and methods of practical organisation.

Hitler did little else while in prison to help the cause of the Nazis. Probably he was reluctant to see the party flourish without him being free to lead it. He bided his time while party colleagues argued among themselves. This was perhaps a dangerous policy for Hitler to pursue, but it did enable him to resume undisputed leadership after his release.

A LOW POINT FOR THE NAZIS

The Nazis, in alliance with other *völkish* parties, won only 14 seats in the Reichstag elections of December 1924. Previously they had 32 representatives. The Nazi Party was virtually destroyed as a coherent organisation. But when Hitler was released on parole in December, he had no serious rival for the leadership. Possible competitors like Röhm were pushed aside. Röhm resigned from the party and was only recalled to lead the SA in 1930. Hitler refounded the party in February 1925, but the process of recovery was slow. The German economy was improving after 1924, and there was at least the appearance of political stability. Support for extremist parties declined. Hitler was banned by anxious authorities from speaking in some German states until 1928. Neverthe-less, he worked to build up party funds, published the second part of *Mein Kampf*, and in 1928 released what became known as *Hitler's Second Book*, with a greater emphasis than before on the author's ideas on foreign policy.

Internal discontent

Hitler faced another problem in the shape of the Strasser brothers. They took the Nazi programme, or at least the Socialist part of it, seriously. They were more popular than Hitler with Nazis in some parts of Germany. There were also internal party grumblings about the extent to which Hitler and a few cronies milked funds and indulged in extravagances such as a large Mercedes.

Hitler relied partly upon a rising star in the party, Josef Goebbels, to fight his corner. Goebbels was a propaganda expert, and as Gauleiter or Nazi leader in Berlin, he occupied a crucial position. Hitler needed help to fight other leading figures in the SA who demonstrated a growing independence, reflecting their opinion of themselves as equals of the purely political leadership. The promotion of the more disciplined and élite SS was Hitler's response to this threat. However, the real crisis in Hitler's relationship with the SA was not to come to a head until 1934.

Hitler himself remained outside the Reichstag. As a foreigner he was ineligible for elections. Although he renounced his Austrian citizenship in 1925, he did not become a German citizen until 1932.

Slow progress

More recent studies, such as Eberhard Kolb's *The Weimar Republic*, have demonstrated convincingly that it is too simplistic to divide the Weimar Republic chronologically into a period of crisis and difficulty up to 1924, followed by one of comparative prosperity and stability under Stresemann between 1924 and 1929. In reality, there were considerable economic and political strains even before the onset of the Depression in 1929. Nevertheless, it is true that progress for Hitler and the Nazi Party was slow after 1924, as the Republic recovered from the trauma of inflation. But slowly and steadily, party membership did grow. The Nazi Party overcame many of its difficulties and internal divisions partly due to the strength of Hitler's personality and leadership – based upon the so-called *Führer-Principle*. The time was fast approaching when Hitler was to become a national figure and a major player in the German political game.

TAKING THE NATIONAL STAGE

Luck certainly played a part in Hitler's progress. The right-wing, more 'respectable' German National Party came to his aid. Its leader from 1928 was Alfred Hugenberg. He controlled vast funds, which he used to subsidise Hitler in the hope of using support for the Nazis on the streets to give his own movement more political clout. Hitler was now able to have his views published in Hugenberg's newspapers all over Germany, and he was able to tap increasingly into the funds of German industrialists and financiers who saw Hitler as a counter to a Communist threat. Hitler soon broke the alliance with Hugenberg, but he had got far more out of the arrangement than had the National Party. The Nazis were beginning to exercise a strong appeal to many of the middle class who felt threatened both by the working class and modern capitalism. But from 1928 Hitler also began to cultivate support among the unemployed.

Stresemann's death in 1929, the Wall Street Crash, and the ensuing world Depression, marked a serious turn of events for the Weimar

Hitler at a party meeting

35

ADOLF – DER ÜBERMENSCH

SCHLUCKT GOLD UND REDET BLECH

*'Adolf the Superman swallows gold and talks crap.' An anti-Nazi cartoon by
John Heartfield, 17 July 1932*

Republic in 1930. It was a turning point in the fortunes of Hitler also. He had always condemned the Weimar Republic as being against Germany's true interests and subservient to Germany's former enemies. The inability of the Republic to cope successfully with the Depression seemed to confirm Hitler's earlier warnings. Nevertheless, Hitler still had to display considerable skill in exploiting the deteriorating political situation which accompanied economic troubles. Hitler became Germany's leader by political manoeuvring, but he was only a key player in the games of political manoeuvre *because* the Nazis were becoming a mass party, and therefore other politicians courted Hitler as a means, so they hoped, of bolstering and furthering their own ambitions.

ALL OR NOTHING

Political deadlock in the Reichstag led to Chancellor Brüning adopting powers to rule by emergency decree after 1930. In the Reichstag elections of that year the Nazis made a big breakthrough, having assiduously cultivated disaffected groups like the farmers. Hitler's propaganda and promises of direct solutions were bearing fruit. He skirted the thin line between insisting that his party would remain true to the democratic process, and hinting that if necessary the Nazi movement would adopt radical tactics. Hitler had to allay the fears of more conservative forces while satisfying the expectations of his more radical supporters. He was aided in this by a combination of luck, his own skills and those of associates like Goebbels, the desperate circumstances of the time, and the machinations and miscalculations of other politicians.

Hitler cultivated important figures in the army in order to allay fears in that quarter that a Nazi takeover would create new opportunities for the SA at the expense of the regular forces. He also maintained his cultivation of business and industrial interests. The electoral successes continued. In the elections of July 1932 the Nazis became the largest parliamentary party. Despite losing a presidential election to Hindenburg – and Hitler did come a creditable second to the revered winner – Hitler was now courted by Franz von Papen and Kurt von Schleicher, who needed Hitler's support to buttress their own precarious positions in the Reichstag.

Hitler's energy was impressive: five major election campaigns between

March and November 1932, flying across Germany and frequently addressing two or three mass meetings a day.

As economic conditions gradually improved, so support for the Nazis peaked and declined. This was evident in the November 1932 elections, although Hitler was still head of the largest party in the Reichstag. However, the difficulty of forming a majority government ensured that Hitler was still the key figure. While restraining impatient factions like the SA, Hitler rejected offers of partnerships or positions such as the Vice-Chancellorship, and held out for the highest post. Hitler was apparently assuming that others would eventually have to accede to his demands, and eventually they did. At any rate, Hitler showed considerable personal courage in holding out for the Chancellorship. Had he failed, the swell of Nazi support, already in decline at the polls, would have rapidly receded further. Some of Hitler's powerful financial supporters were beginning to have second thoughts about the Nazis, and some in the party like Gregor Strasser were prepared to compromise for a share in office.

Papen secured the offer of the Chancellorship for Hitler in January 1933. Hindenburg was persuaded to agree. But the assumption on Papen's part was that Hitler would be dominated by non-Nazi colleagues in the Cabinet.

There was no inevitability about the events of January 1933. It was fortunate for Hitler that not just a group of scheming politicians came to his aid, but also that important sections of German industry still regarded the Nazis as the best alternative to the Weimar Republic or a possible Communist takeover. There were few prepared to defend the Republic. The Communists mistakenly believed that the rise of Hitler was a temporary phenomenon, signalling the imminent collapse of capitalism. The Social Democrats and the Centre Party had had their fling. Their organisations were to be dissolved in 1933 without overt resistance. The outcomes of the political manoeuvrings of the months before January 1933 were not inevitable; on the other hand there were few in Germany at the time of Hitler's appointment ready to lament the imminent passing of parliamentary democracy, even if they could not anticipate the radical changes of the months ahead.

timeline	1924	Hitler in prison. *Mein Kampf* written
	1925	The Nazi Party re-founded
	1929	Wall Street Crash and onset of Depression
	1930	Brüning became Chancellor
		Nazi breakthrough in Reichstag elections
	1932 April	Hindenburg defeated Hitler in presidential election
	May	Papen became Chancellor
	July	Further Nazi successes in Reichstag elections
	November	Drop in Nazi support in Reichstag elections
	December	Schleicher appointed Chancellor
	1933 January	Hitler appointed Chancellor

Points to consider

1) How valuable is *Mein Kampf* for an understanding of Hitler's beliefs and attitudes?
2) How skilfully did Hitler lead the Nazi Party after the failure of the Munich Putsch, and how successfully did he exploit conditions inside Germany between 1929 and 1933?
3) Did Hitler come to power by backstairs intrigue or popular support?

4

FÜHRER, 1933–9

CONSOLIDATION

The new leader of Germany was an unprepossessing individual at first sight. He was five feet and nine inches tall and weighed 150 pounds. His legs were unusually short and his gait was awkward, as he dragged his left foot slightly behind him. Hitler was self-conscious about his bad teeth, and his moustache was designed to lessen the impact of his large nose. But it was Hitler's political potential that interested Germany's élite. The appointment of Hitler as Chancellor in January 1933 was seen by some of his Conservative allies as an opportunity to use his mass support for their own Nationalist ends. For Hitler, it was but the beginning of a process by which real or potential opposition was crushed, as the Nazi Party asserted its control over Germany. He became less and less dependent upon the party. Hitler's power was essentially personal rather than deriving from any office that he held. Likewise, the authority of other leading Nazis depended less upon their official positions than upon the closeness of their relationship with Hitler, and their ease of access to his presence. The exercise of Hitler's power, the *Führer-Principle*, was to be arbitrary precisely because it was largely determined by personal whim rather than by institutional factors.

The period from January 1933 to August 1934 saw the replacement of the Weimar Republic by a one party state. Hitler saw this state as an instrument of coercion directed against enemies from within and without Germany. To what extent the consolidation of power can be equated with Hitler's personal dictatorship will be explored later. What is beyond dispute is that the process of consolidation was relatively smooth. This can be explained partly by the fact that all potential opposition to the Nazis on both left and right was divided and, in many instances, unable to appreciate the potential danger from the Nazis.

The Reichstag building was burned to the ground soon after Hitler's appointment as Chancellor. Whoever was responsible for this outrage, it was used by Hitler to stir up fears of a Communist revolution in Germany. Although the Nazis did not acquire an absolute majority in the Reichstag elections which followed, by excluding Communist deputies and intimidating other parties, Hitler was able to secure an Enabling Law giving him the legal basis for dictatorship. He was provided with full legislative and executive powers. There followed a series of measures all designed to remove centres of potential opposition: the subordination of state governments to Berlin; the abolition of unions and other political parties; an agreement with the Catholic Church; a rapid takeover of the media and the educational system. This was not achieved by force and intimidation alone. Part of Hitler's success was to attract many Germans through the image of dynamism projected by the Nazis, and through a succession of rather vague promises about national regeneration, rather than specific plans. Behind the scenes Hitler busied himself with neutralising, or in some cases gaining the support of, powerful forces within the army and industry. Meanwhile the Nazi Party got on with the business of transforming the ideology of the German population, to make it readier to accept both Nazi philosophy and specific measures.

THE 1934 PURGE

There had been an anti-capitalist strain in the young Nazi Party, and there were Nazis at all levels who welcomed the prospect of radical economic and social change upon grasping power in 1933. However, it is doubtful whether Hitler ever intended a genuine social revolution of the type hoped for by some of his more radical supporters. His priorities were the consolidation of power and military expansion. In terms of administrative changes, there were also practical difficulties to be overcome. Unlike the Communists in Russia in 1917, who had inherited a state in which powerful bureaucracies and centres of influence had been destroyed, Germany in 1933 was a country in which vested interests were still a force. The existing bureaucracy could be infiltrated by the Nazis but not destroyed overnight. In any case, for all his contempt for the old Establishment, Hitler had no intention of destroying organisations which would be necessary to his plans for making Germany great. He certainly did not want the professional army absorbed into an SA-dominated revolutionary people's militia. Hitler's gods were order and power. If it was necessary to crush the hopes of his radical supporters who wanted to turn Germany upside down, Hitler would have no compunction about doing so.

By early 1934 Hitler was already committed to an expansion of the regular army and a concentration upon rearmament. He also awaited the death of the aged President Hindenburg in order to consolidate his own power and preclude any last-ditch attempt by Conservatives to replace the Chancellor. Röhm and his ambitions for the SA were a threat. Hitler was egged on by other Nazis who themselves were fearful of Röhm's power, and the army itself was happy to see the overthrow of a powerful rival. Thus fear, ambition and personal rivalries came together in the ruthless 'Night of the Long Knives' of June 1934. During this Purge, not only was Röhm liquidated, but potentially influential Conservatives and Nazis such as Gregor Strasser were eliminated. The latter had made the mistake of taking the original Nazi Party programme seriously.

Hitler justified his bloodletting by claiming to have nipped a second revolution in the bud. In a time of 'national crisis' he had acted decisively in the interests of state security. There were enough Germans to tacitly support his actions or to have the sense to keep quiet.

On Hindenburg's death shortly afterwards, Hitler took over the presidency and declared himself Führer (Leader). In future, if there were to be any major changes, they would be initiated by Hitler, not forced upon him by radicals from below. Alan Bullock saw the crisis of 1934 as an example of how Hitler was able to manage a difficult situation in an opportunistic way, while pursuing a longer-term programme to strengthen his power. The crisis 'shows how firm a grasp he had of the way in which opportunities could be fitted into the end in view, turning what could have been a self-inflicted disaster for him and the Nazi Party into a personal triumph which placed him above both Party and state.' (*Parallel Lives*, pp. 385–6).

HITLER'S REICH

Hitler may have been optimistic about his prospects for achieving power, but he had given little thought to how exactly he would exercise that power within Germany. At any rate, he had no specific plan. Although Nazis were infiltrated into important positions and institutions, there was no radical overhaul of existing bureaucracies. Hitler took a great interest in minutiae, for example he astonished army professionals by his technical knowledge of weaponry. He was equally fond of generalising about grand strategy and grandiose concepts like the 'Thousand Year Reich', but he did not show much inclination to concern himself with the intermediate sphere: the nuts and bolts of government and bureaucratic structures which bind modern States together. The Nazis did make some innovations, notably the establishment of regional Gau (districts) under powerful Gauleiters, to replace the old federal structure, but in most instances they left established structures in place or added to them. The Reichstag was preserved as a stage upon which Hitler could make pronouncements, especially on foreign policy. Also the Reichsrat, representing the *Länder* or states, remained in being. This was the constitutional façade hiding Hitler's dictatorship.

Administration

In Hitler's Reich there was no coherent administrative structure nor even a straightforward chain of command. Germany was certainly not as monolithic or authoritarian a state as was believed at the time and later, particularly by those superficially impressed by notions of German 'efficiency'. Obviously the Nazi Party was powerful, and it had an important role in influencing ordinary Germans through organisations like the Hitler Youth, but the party's relationship with the State was ambiguous. If Hitler wanted a particular task carried out, he sometimes created a special agency. This was to be the case with the Four-Year Plan Organisation, which could operate independently of the government.

Was it that Hitler could not be bothered to create an efficient system of government, or did he simply prefer there to be institutions and individuals competing for power and influence, since paradoxically this could strengthen his own position as Führer? Because there were no clear-cut lines of command, it was difficult as well as dangerous to challenge Hitler. He could intervene at will, although he was lazy about administrative matters and left subordinates like Himmler to develop their own mini-empires. This may have been, in part at least, a calculated laziness, or an arrogance which assumed that he was unchallengeable, and was therefore safe in letting subordinates vie for influence beneath him.

Hitler was not interested in genuine discussion. There were twelve Cabinet meetings in 1935, four in 1936 and six in 1937. The last Cabinet meeting was held in February 1938. Formal votes were not taken. Hitler issued edicts from his Chancellery: all that was required was his own signature. A minister who secured Hitler's signature did not have to consult other ministers. Hitler did not allow each of his subordinates to know more than was absolutely necessary. With his 'personal' system of power, Hitler was untrammelled by the bureaucratic checks and balances to which the old governing élite had been subject.

Hitler's role

A controversy has developed around the issue of Hitler's exact role in the Third Reich. The German historian Bracher took the view that Hitler's method of 'divide and rule' largely accounts for the bureaucratic chaos described earlier. Hitler was closely identified with the Nazi state. This is often called the 'intentionalist' interpretation of Hitler's rule. In contrast, some 'structuralist' historians have preferred to study the structures of the Nazi state rather than focusing upon Hitler. Some of these historians saw the existence of competing bureaucracies not as a 'plot' created by Hitler, but a state of affairs brought about by Hitler's lack of interest in systematising his government. This interpretation is perhaps more convincing than the notion of a deliberate 'divide and rule' policy. Hitler had no need of the latter: there might be different cliques and factions within the Nazi movement, but there was nobody trying to replace Hitler. The Strasser brothers and Ernst Röhm had been attempting to win Hitler over to their point of view, not to usurp his position.

It is quite possible to interpret Hitler's role in varying ways in different contexts. For example, Hitler blocked schemes to rationalise the governmental structure, possibly out of distrust at any move which

might have the effect of restrictin
individuals, such as Robert Ley an
develop huge power bases of their
colleagues – like most politicians
blind eye to their activities, ev
notions of government. There v
disputes, notably when he s
government ministries over
aloof. Whether this was a delib...
advantage for Hitler. Popular perceptions
were frequent grumblings about the activities
government, he himself was spared criticism by the mass of Ge...

As Ian Kershaw emphasised, it would be misleading to characterise
Hitler as a 'weak' dictator. Arbitary, yes, since Hitler sometimes acted
upon impulse. Even Goebbels referred to Hitler's 'weakness' in his diary:

> We live in a state where areas of authority have been unclearly
> divided . . . the consequence is a complete lack of direction in
> German domestic policy . . . From this developed most of the
> quarrels between the real leaders and ruling authorities.

However, this was written in March 1943, when Hitler was
preoccupied with matters of war. If Hitler ever appeared 'weak', it was
rather a reluctance to become too involved in the day-to-day
practicalities of government. When he *did* want his way, he got it. There
are no examples of major policy decisions by Hitler being successfully
blocked by subordinates. This was particularly true in foreign policy.
But even in domestic affairs, there is no convincing evidence that Hitler
was unhappy with the direction of events – it would be misleading to talk
about a coherent social and economic policy – or that he could not have
intervened more dramatically had he so wished. It is true that when
Hitler made decisions he often remained anxious for days afterwards and
sought reassurance. But although he might hesitate and agonise, he did
act, so he cannot be accused of lacking firmness of purpose.

ECONOMIC POLICY

It was long held that Hitler did not have a detailed or coherent economic
policy in 1933. He took the praise for Germany's economic recovery,

way when he was appointed Chancellor. Hitler
as supporting the peasantry and rearmament,
subordinates like Schacht and Göring to implement

has been made of Hitler's supposed 'ignorance' of
it was more a case of his disagreeing with the experts, and
deliberately ignoring accepted economic maxims. The Nazis
bated economic strategies before 1933, and were ready to
iment with interventionist policies not dissimilar to some of those of
e great English economist Keynes.

Hitler's decision in 1933 to link further economic recovery to military
expansion was a calculated one. The largely orthodox Schacht directed
policy. He made rearmament possible by securing credit, but became
disillusioned when he realised that Hitler intended to continue with a
programme of full rearmament *after* the economy had recovered. The
existing policy did not produce rapid enough results for Hitler. Göring
was given powers in 1936 to implement a programme of autarky, to free
Germany from dependence on other countries. Even so, the Four-Year
Plan was but a pale reflection of the Soviet Five-Year version.

Hitler allowed more pressure to be put on the economy, a dangerous
policy according to the experts. But again, this was not ignorance on
Hitler's part, simply a consequence of his belief that when a successful
war was eventually fought, the resources of the defeated opponents could
be used to rebuild and bolster the German economy. The assumption
was made that Germany *would* be victorious, and the resulting New
Order would provide the master race with a high standard of living at
the expense of the defeated peoples of the East. A successful war would
certainly be crucial, if Hitler meant what he told his generals: in
August 1939 he warned them that the German economy would be in a
serious condition within a few years. Some historians, including Mason,
have concluded from this that economic concerns were an important
factor in determining the moment of hostilities, although this theory has
far from universal acceptance.

Although expenditure on rearmament rose, the economy was not
totally geared to war. Hitler was too aware of the social implications of a
rigidly controlled war economy to have gone as far as Stalin in creating a
siege mentality or, on the other hand, to have made himself a slave of big
business. When war actually came, plans for labour mobilisation were

modified in response to reports of worker unrest, and there was to be considerable reluctance to mobilise women at all. Drastic austerity measures were avoided lest they turn the population against the Nazis.

The debate over the nature of Germany's preparations for war has excited considerable historical controversy. Hitler was certainly involved in the rearmament debate at the time. He chose rearmament 'in width' rather than 'in depth', since the former approach required fewer economic resources, and also accorded with Hitler's own predilection for a short decisive war. Less economic dislocation also reduced the likelihood of unrest among the German population, whose living standards would suffer if massive amounts of resources were channelled into supplying the Armed Forces. It was only after the failure of Blitzkrieg, or 'lightning war', in 1941–2 that Speer, as Armaments Minister, was allowed to mobilise the economy for war, to the extent of restricting the output of consumer goods in favour of arms. Only then was it accepted that guns came before butter – a decision which was to prolong the war, but came too late to actually decide it in Germany's favour.

Nazi economic measures such as Göring's Four-Year Plan resulted in a kind of 'controlled' capitalism: the Nazis held sway, but individual businessmen enjoyed influence and profits. Hitler wanted rearmament, but there were contradictory pressures at work. For example, while Hitler spoke enthusiastically about preserving the peasantry and expressed a marked distaste for the impact of urbanisation, he also supported big business. He was not one of those 'Green' Nazis who hated all industry as a corrupting, evil force; he enthused about technological progress and had a strictly utilitarian view of economics generally. Economic progress was to be welcomed as a means of gaining workers' support for his Nationalist policies.

During the second half of the war, when total war required a more strenuous economic effort, Albert Speer did implement a more co-ordinated programme, but efforts to rationalise and increase production, while successful in many cases, were still bedevilled by inefficiencies, redtape, and the competing activities of semi-independent organisations like the SS. The Soviet Five-Year Plans were not models of efficiency, but they were, nevertheless, far more coherent than Nazi planning efforts.

HITLER'S 'FOLK COMMUNITY'

Hitler was more interested in the social and cultural condition of the German people than in economic theories. He was fond of expounding his prejudices – on education, on the role of women, on race, and so on. Although as with the economy and political structures, there was not a coherent or at least consistent policy, it is possible to identify Hitler's imprint upon many aspects of the Third Reich. For example, his ideas on the 'Folk Community' and the importance of physical fitness were reflected in the youth organisations and school syllabuses. Sometimes pragmatism won at the expense of ideology: Hitler's preference for women in the home as childbearers restricted progress in their social liberation, but eventually during wartime women were employed in the labour force on a large scale.

ANTI-SEMITISM IN ACTION

Ideology was surely the driving force behind Nazi measures against the Jews. It is certainly the 'intentionalist' argument that Hitler's racial ideology was central to the Holocaust, the attempted extermination of Europe's Jews, with a clear line of continuity between his racist outpourings in the early 1920s and the actual policies of the 1940s. Hildebrand talks of the 'fundamental' importance of Hitler's racism. Opposing this interpretation, the 'functionalists' point to the absence of a clear Führer Order relating to the Holocaust, and the latter is seen as the result of a cumulative process of radicalisation of beliefs and improvised measures. Martin Broszat stresses the importance of individual initiative down to 1942, and sees the more formalised programme as taking shape only when the leadership found itself unable to cope with huge numbers of Jews on its hands in the occupied territories. Such arguments are sometimes reinforced by reference to the apparent vagueness of many of Hitler's racist comments in his early speeches and writings, full of venom but short on actual detail of his intentions.

It is not incumbent upon us to accept either of these two extreme views in their totality. There *were* times, notably in the early 1920s, when anti-Marxist sentiments seemed more important in Nazi pronouncements than anti-Semitism, although Communism and

Judaism were often linked in Nazi propaganda. Nor can the fact that Hitler often expressed violent 'intentions' towards the Jews be taken as absolute proof that he instigated the extermination programme several years later.

However, anti-Semitism was certainly crucial in Nazi ideology. It did not necessarily readily translate itself into detailed and practical policies. Hitler himself admitted once that there was no such thing as a pure 'race', for all the talk of Aryan or Nordic superiority. But the ideology was significant. It may be that depriving Jews of citizenship and property rights was viewed by some Germans as a means of making a profit. It is certainly true that some Nazis, both powerful and less prominent, were more fiercely anti-Semitic in their utterances than Hitler himself. It *is* difficult to believe that Hitler was not also committed to anti-Jewish measures for ideological and political reasons. To argue otherwise would be to fly in the face of all Hitler's private as well as public utterances, in addition to the attitudes he displayed in his youth. This is not to say that the Holocaust was planned well in advance.

The anti-Jewish measures came in stages. In 1933 there was a boycott of Jewish shops. In 1935 the Nuremberg Laws deprived the Jews of citizenship and protection. In 1938 the synagogues were burned down on *Kristallnacht*. Can these events be construed as constituting a deliberate plan?

Extermination of the Jews

Alan Bullock claimed that there was no *official* persecution of the Jews early in 1933 because Hitler was concerned not to arouse opposition abroad or to tarnish the image of his 'legal' takeover of power; and that agreeing to a boycott of Jewish businesses was a concession to radical Nazis who were champing at the bit to do something even more drastic. However, by 1941 the Germans were in territorial control of much of Western and Eastern Europe, and they were responsible for millions of Jews with no practical way of expelling them. The 'Final Solution', the decision to exterminate the Jews, was implemented through individuals including Heydrich, Göring and Himmler, and was formalised at the Wannsee Conference of January 1942. Hitler was not present at this Conference, although Heydrich was. It is difficult to agree with David Irving that the extermination was at first carried out by Himmler without Hitler's knowledge, a claim which Irving uses to support his argument that Hitler increasingly lost control over his subordinates. A Hitler directive does not exist. But there is no reason why we should expect detailed orders from Hitler to have survived, although there has been considerable speculation about a 'secret' Hitler directive supposedly issued in 1941 after the invasion of Russia. This was 'concerned' with beginning the extermination of the Jews. In 1941 Göring *did* issue a directive to Heydrich to prepare for a 'Final Solution'. Did Hitler give prior approval to this order? Hitler's subordinates and Gauleiters had the power to initiate drastic measures without Hitler's direct orders. But this was a major operation. Did Hitler really not know?

Whether Hitler did initiate the movement towards large-scale killings in 1941 and 1942 or not, he was surely aware of what was happening and gave at the very least his tacit consent, or even a verbal order. His approval surely accounts also for the continuation of the extermination programme long after it was clear that the war was lost.

STYLE AND LEADERSHIP
—

Discussion of Hitler and the Holocaust brings us back to the question of Hitler's leadership, or lack of it, and his tactics and strategy. It is possible to become bogged down in an argument about the extent to which Hitler was an opportunist or a pragmatist. Did he seize the moment when it presented itself, or did he pursue long-term goals? Did he do both? This debate will certainly emerge when we consider Hitler's foreign policy. There is a middle way. Many politicians have specific objectives, but are flexible in the way in which they prioritise them and pursue a particular aim at a particular time. There were times in the 1930s when Hitler was preoccupied with foreign policy. After 1939 he was preoccupied with war. This did not preclude an interest in other matters, but they may have taken second place. Similarly, a reluctance to engage in detail, a charge often levelled against Hitler, may not be laziness but a belief that the leader's job is to make policy while subordinates hammer out the details. Another factor in the equation was Hitler's unpredictability, combined sometimes with a reluctance to take decisions as opposed to waiting on events. Put together, these attributes go towards the make-up of a complex personality or style of leadership. Thus any interpretation which labels Hitler simply as 'opportunistic', 'lazy' or 'crazed' is bound to be simplistic.

DREAMS AND REALITY

What of Hitler the dictator and the man, at the height of his power within Germany? There is ample record of Hitler's own musings, particularly at the time of his accession to power, and in 1941–2, the *Table Talk* period, when Hitler rambled on a range of subjects before devoted listeners.

Hitler's ideas were a peculiar hotch-potch, deriving from his own life, his reading, his prejudices, and his visions for the future. They ranged over all topics, and were frequently very banal. Although Bullock and others have drawn attention to Hitler's capacity for self-dramatisation, his actor's ability to project himself into a role, to suddenly lose his temper and then to regain his self-control, we can assume that Hitler generally meant what he said, at least when talking in private.

LIFESTYLE OF A DICTATOR

Hitler relied upon certain key subordinates to relieve him from the tedium of the nuts and bolts of administration. Hess and later Bormann were two such subordinates, the latter being Head of the Party Chancellery. Hitler preferred to deal with individuals rather than committees. Subordinates soon learned that there were certain ways by which his interest or involvement could be won or alienated, for example he refused to read long reports. According to Bullock:

> the art of politics in the Third Reich reduced itself to being the last man to catch Hitler's attention, informally, anywhere, at any time, and hoping (often with good reason) that Hitler would say 'Agreed', leaving it to ministers, civil servants and party bosses to fight over exactly what he had agreed to.
>
> (*Parallel Lives*, p. 423)

Some actions arose directly from Hitler's own initiatives, including some relatively early in his chancellorship: the Treaty with Poland and the Anglo–German Naval Treaty, for example.

Hitler's lifestyle as Chancellor was quite frugal. He was rich from the royalties from *Mein Kampf* and revenue from having his portrait on stamps. But he had a small personal staff to administer his own affairs.

This staff included Julius Schreck, the first leader of the SS and Hitler's chauffeur until his death in 1936; his bodyguard Julius Schaub; William Brückner, his Chief Adjutant from 1935 to 1941; and Hitler's old commanding officer, Fritz Widemann, on the staff between 1935 and 1939. Such men became less influential as Bormann's power grew. Starting as Chief of Staff to Hess, Bormann increasingly controlled access to Hitler.

NAZI COLLEAGUES

Göring, Himmler and Goebbels were three well-known Nazis who were powerful in their own right. They were privileged in having frequent access to Hitler. Göring was the least obsessed with questions of ideology, being more interested in power for its own sake. There were a few other 'Old Fighters', Nazis from the early days of the movement, whose names were less well known, but who were, nevertheless, part of Hitler's entourage and frequently in his company. These men included Franz Schwarz, the party Treasurer; Fritz Sauckel, Gauleiter of Thuringia; Erich Koch, Gauleiter of East Prussia; Karl Kaufmann, Gauleiter of Hamburg; and Josef Bürchel, a Reich Commissioner. Some army officers also had regular access to Hitler in order to facilitate his liaison with the Armed Forces. However, Hitler felt most at home with a few individuals like the party photographer Hoffmann, his architect Albert Speer, his doctor Morell, and the faithful Eva Braun.

Some of Hitler's associates were simply unequal to their responsibilities. Ribbentrop, an ambassador and then Foreign Minister, was one such example. He was one of those given special missions, in his case to establish contacts abroad. Hitler was often tolerant of faults in his entourage. Old colleagues in particular could often expect to have their deficiencies overlooked. Hitler was conservative in personal relations and matters of daily routine, and disliked changes in personnel. He showed far more loyalty to colleagues and immediate subordinates than his rival dictator Stalin. In return, Hitler succeeded in retaining his charismatic hold over most of his subordinates, who seemed genuinely to believe in his genius.

Hitler was confident that he could sum up an individual's characteristics very quickly. There were those who were immune to his own particular brand of charisma, and he tended to avoid them. Apart from his associates, Hitler had little trust in others. This was reflected in his practice of keeping three coloured pencils on his desk. These were used to mark documents not according to their content, but according to the degree to which he trusted the author.

LIFE WITH THE FÜHRER

Hitler's idiosyncratic style of government was reflected in his physical surroundings. His favourite residence was the Berghof, constructed in the 1930s. Well away from Berlin, and in the mountains where Hitler could enjoy the solitude for which he frequently craved, he could indulge his dreams and live his life of routine. That routine was soon well established. At about 10 a.m. Hitler read the newspapers and brief reports in bed. At 11 a.m. he breakfasted and read more reports. At midday he finally emerged to meet colleagues, visitors or advisors. Lunch was served late, and might last for up to three hours between 2 and 5 p.m. Gauleiters and other leading Nazis would often be present at lunch, but not army officers. Lunch was a lengthy affair mainly because Hitler enjoyed talking at length.

Supper, at about 8 p.m. might be followed by an hour's rest. Then watching films or indulging in lengthy monologues might continue the entertainment until Hitler retired at 3 or 4 a.m.

HEALTH

Hitler's lifestyle was scarcely healthy. From 1937 he took no regular exercise; by then he was already suffering from stomach pains, and was generally concerned about his health. His ailments have been variously ascribed to the stress of office, his vegetarianism, or straightforward hypochondria. There was almost certainly a strong dose of the latter in Hitler. He was convinced that he had heart disease. In 1936 he met Doctor Theodor Morell who became his personal physician, and has generally had a bad press from historians. His many pills and potions have been dismissed as quackery, or labelled as positively harmful, even to the extent of slowly poisoning the Führer. They did contain potentially lethal substances such as strychnine and strophine. However, Hitler claimed to feel better for Morell's drugs, and it is true that Morell did not have an easy task in ministering to Hitler, who distrusted all experts in any field.

In 1941 Hitler became seriously ill, when the pressure of exercising leadership in the war may have begun to take its toll. The state of Hitler's health must be of interest to historians, since it *may* have affected his policies. It is certainly true that Hitler was convinced that he must fulfil many of his ambitions for Germany while he was still capable of leadership. Did this hasten his efforts to create a Greater Germany? His physical deterioration may have affected his judgement later in the war, although it is impossible to relate any particular incident to a landmark in Hitler's health.

Concern about his well-being encompassed his diet. Breakfast might consist of milk, tea, fruit, and in his later years, cake and drinking chocolate. Lunch comprised soup, fruit and vegetarian fare. Although Hitler was full of prejudices, he did not inflict his dietary beliefs upon his companions, who were allowed meat. He also ate fried food, dumplings, cheese and eggs, but was mostly teetotal, and would not allow smoking in his presence.

Hitler developed particular personal habits, such as an overscrupulous concern for personal hygiene. He constantly washed his hands. His obsessively consistent regime included having his valet record the speed at which he could dress and undress himself.

THE FÜHRER'S THOUGHTS

Hitler's intimates might have few dietary restrictions with which to contend, but they did, nevertheless, suffer an uncomfortable lifestyle in the Berghof. They could be the butt of Hitler's liking for cruel practical jokes. This may tell us something about Hitler's character, although we need not go so far as Robert Waite in projecting Hitler's delight in 'terrifying' his friends on to a need to exact revenge on those who had terrified him in his youth – after all, Hitler's early life had not been that unpleasant.

Goebbels had an acerbic wit which he employed in Hitler's presence. Other visitors, however, were expected mostly to listen to Hitler's monologues. Perhaps they did not mind, since Hitler was careful to surround himself in private with those who had no original opinions or those who could not challenge his ascendancy. Psychoanalysts have related this trait to Hitler's insecurity, which led him to fear those who knew more than himself. The intelligent Speer was an exception, possibly because Hitler saw in him the architectural genius he himself had once hoped to become.

Hitler generally talked, others listened. On the few occasions when Hitler was silent, he brooded rather than listen to others. Because his opinions were not challenged, he maintained his convictions and prejudices to the end. This was ironic given his own claim to be an original thinker. Hitler simply did not understand the concept of genuine discussion.

HITLER'S WOMEN

Hitler's constant companion at the Berghof was Eva Braun, but she was not the first important woman in his adult life. In the late 1920s he had been infatuated with his niece, Geli Raubel. She was 19 years younger than the future Führer. She was possibly pregnant by Hitler, and commited suicide in 1931. Her death prompted suicidal thoughts in her distraught uncle.

Eva Braun was an assistant to the party photographer, Hoffman, and became Hitler's mistress in 1932. Eva made her own attempts at suicide in 1932 and 1935, but was devoted to Hitler. She remains a somewhat shadowy figure, without great intelligence. Hitler kept her firmly in the background. Like Geli Raubel, Eva's life was dictated by the Führer, who forbade them both to dance and smoke, and refused to let them appear in public. Hitler was well aware of the hysterical reaction he evoked in women in his public persona, and the political advantages which thereby accrued. He used this fact to justify his staying single, until 1945, when he married the faithful Eva shortly before their deaths. Until then Hitler had always insisted that he was 'married to Germany'.

One talented woman who was attracted to Hitler was the film-maker Leni Riefenstahl. She helped to promote the 'Führer image', notably in her documentary *Triumph of the Will*, a glorification of the Nuremberg Party Rallies.

Hitler's attitude towards women was paradoxical: he was generally contemptuous of them, but enjoyed being in the presence of beautiful women. Both contemporaries and historians have disputed as to whether Hitler experienced a 'normal' sex life. He regarded women as false and fickle, and those around him he required to be neither intelligent nor original, nor have the temerity to argue with him. As he said, 'I have enough ideas for both'. Yet he was anxious to convince women of his virility. A young woman who visited the Obersalzberg was startled when Hitler suddenly proffered the Nazi salute and roared:

> I can hold my arm like that for two solid hours. I never feel tired when my storm troopers and soldiers march past me and I stand at this salute. I never move. My arm is like granite – rigid and unbending. But Göring can't stand it. He has to drop his hand after half an hour of this salute. He's flabby. But I am hard. For two hours I can keep my arm stretched out in the salute. That is four times as long as Göring. That means I'm four times stronger than Göring. It's an amazing feat. I marvel at my own power.

For all Hitler's contempt and desire to impress, he also fully subscribed to the Nazis' projected ideal of women as faithful wives and mothers, fighting their own battle on behalf of the master race by bringing new Aryan babies into the world. Hitler's standards were exacting. His staff were required to get his permission before they were married. Once the knot was tied, Hitler expected each couple to have four children.

Psychoanalysts have argued that Hitler feared women. If that was so, he also used them to great political advantage. He drew a famous comparison between the 'crowd' and women, and worked on a crowd as if seducing a woman. If the masses became a kind of sexual substitute for Hitler, it helps to explain the emotional intensity of his public speechmaking.

'A RARE GENIUS'

Given Hitler's reluctance to engage in day-to-day administration, it is not surprising that he found ample time to indulge himself and either impress or bore his associates with his views on a wide range of topics. Albert Speer wrote that Hitler's intellectual development stopped in the Vienna of 1910. His opinions remained, thereafter, inflexible. Hitler was fully aware of the fact and proud of it. Opposition to his views on anything simply increased his own dogmatism. There was unconscious irony in this, given that he also saw himself as an artist and a consummate thinker, one who could afford to despise experts, to whom he refused to listen. Hitler quite simply regarded himself as one of the rare geniuses of history.

The arts

Architecture was the most important of the arts to Hitler. As in most things, his taste in architecture was geared to the period before 1914. Hitler favoured huge architectural projects: the German people would be able to look up at the results, and this would have the political advantage of helping to consolidate his regime.

In the arts generally, Hitler recognised nothing of genius from the twentieth century – he admired the achievements of Greek and Roman antiquity. For Hitler, the Romans had contributed more to history than the early Germans.

Hitler's tastes in music were very specific. His favourite composers were Wagner, Grieg and Bruckner. He generally preferred German artists and composers. He considered himself 'the most musical of all Germans', and in 1945 was to rule Himmler out of the reckoning as a possible successor on the eccentric grounds that he was not musical enough!

Also typically dogmatic in the field of the visual arts, Hitler was filled with fury by modern and abstract art: 'Anyone who sees and paints a sky green and pastures blue ought to be sterilised.'

Hitler continued to read voraciously after coming to power. His reading was mostly utilitarian. In order to grasp the main content quickly, he would read from back to front.

For all his boasting about his artistic temperament, Hitler's views were completely rigid and lacking all humanity. In the words of Trevor-Roper:

> His ultimate conception of German culture is so utterly revolting. To him it was simply a question of more cakes for Germans and less for non-Germans. He was a complete and rigid materialist.
>
> (*Hitler's Table Talk*, p. xxxiii)

History

Although many of Hitler's views on history were eccentric, they were important in influencing his actions. Hitler regarded himself as one of the few key figures in history, recognising few others. He did accept that Bismarck had been the most important historical figure of the nineteenth century, but he showed no particular interest in Bismarck's writings. Racial nonsense pervaded much of Hitler's own thinking. He believed that nations such as Britain and the United States had achieved greatness largely because of a strain of German blood in their peoples – although at other times Hitler proclaimed that the United States, as a multi-ethnic nation, could not compete with an 'Aryan' Germany. Hitler's reading of history was very selective, and he had none of the professional historian's reluctance to make dogmatic assertions without any possibility of later revision in the light of new evidence or orthodoxies. Dogmatism was allied to a utilitarian interpretation of history: Hitler ascribed the decline of ancient classical civilisation to the degenerative effect of Christianity – hardly an original notion. But he went on to claim that modern European civilisation was threatened anew from the East. This time the threat was in the form of Jewish Bolshevism. The German people, a race which was 'the combined product of violence, ideas from antiquity, and Christianity', would play a leading role in resisting this threat. Since this mission was of historic importance, Hitler had no time for human weakness: the weak would go to the wall, and deservedly so.

This 'world view' of history was the result of Hitler's amateurish, prejudiced, scientific 'understanding'. His particular interest in biology and Darwinism translated neatly into notions of survival of the fittest, a concept which Hitler applied to peoples and nations.

Providence

What was Hitler's perception of his own place in this scheme of things? He had been chosen by Providence to lead the Germans in their struggle for national existence. Hitler sometimes agonised over decisions, but he was generally self-confident precisely because he was convinced that he *was* a tool of Providence. This conviction also allowed him to eschew all normal moral considerations, since the demands of the nation state transcended all individual human 'rights'.

Contrary to popular belief, Hitler was not anti-religious as such. He despised the Christian Church, certainly, although Catholics received a smaller share of his contempt than Protestants. He was prepared to accept the greatness of an 'Aryan' Christ. He also had some respect for the position of the Church as a powerful force in history, if not as a system of belief. Hitler did become progressively more hostile towards the Churches, but he retained his belief in Providence.

The world at large

Hitler's confidence in German superiority was partly the result of his sheer ignorance of the wider world. He had read widely, but seldom travelled outside Germany's borders. He relied for information mostly on films and reports. During the Second World War he watched only newsreels, up to the Battle of Stalingrad in 1942. But before 1939, and again after 1942, he watched French and British films, and read French and English magazines – Hitler was not as ignorant of foreign languages as is commonly assumed. Hitler's two favourite films were *Snow White* and *King Kong*; his favourite actress was the child star Shirley Temple.

Hitler had a long list of pet hates. It included the aristocracy, royalty, intellectuals generally, teachers, lawyers, freemasons and priests. He also held very strong views on foreign statesmen. He admired Stalin greatly as a leader who pursued those goals which he set himself with absolute ruthlessness. But Hitler came to despise other contemporary leaders, notably Churchill and Roosevelt. His feelings for Mussolini veered between admiration, contempt, and even affection. Ironically for one who was sceptical about the good intentions of others, Hitler never doubted his own professions of 'statesmanship'.

Nowhere did Hitler's tendency to stereotype display itself more clearly than in his love–hate relationship with the British. Hitler admired Henry VIII and Oliver Cromwell as the only two positive individuals in British history, although he praised T. E. Lawrence's *Seven Pillars Of Wisdom*. The British had at least succeeded in building an empire: '[The British] are incomparably insolent, but I admire them nonetheless. We still have a lot to learn from them.'

THE SUPREME ORATOR

In his public oratory Hitler's range of topics was considerably narrower than in his private monologues, but his prejudices were still on display. Alan Bullock described Hitler's faults as an orator as speaking for too long, of being verbose and repetitive, of beginning his speeches awkwardly and ending them abruptly. But he also emphasised his intensity, his apparent sincerity, and above all Hitler's ability to put into words what was already in the minds of his audience – a reassuring process both for his audience and himself.

When talking to people, Hitler judged them by their hands or eyes. His own eyes, light-blue and intense, had an almost hypnotic effect on individuals. Hitler knew this, and frequently stared people down. When speaking to crowds, as for example at the Nuremberg Party Rallies, the techniques were different. Film of Hitler speaking on public occasions fails to convey his full impact upon an audience. We are not predisposed to respond or believe because we have not lived in the climate of propaganda and Führer-worship. We were not physically present to be influenced by the psychology of the crowd, and we have not witnessed the whole, lengthy performance. Even those who *were* there and *did* listen were not always won over. Back in 1927 a critic wrote:

> Hitler is an orator. And yet his command of rhetoric, his art of arranging and constructing his speech and leading up to his main points in a logical sequence, is very limited. It also lacks the best seasoning – humour. Hitler is wholly humourless, just bombastic. His climaxes consist in a redoubling of the bombast . . . Rhetorically weak, thought-content nil; there only remains, as the most effective factor in Hitler's speech, his capacity to convey transports of feeling.

Yet it was those very 'transports of feeling' that so delighed most of the crowd. Frequently Hitler would emphasise certain words or themes over and over again in order to hammer home his message.

The American psychoanalyst Erich Fromm, in *Escape From Freedom*, commented upon the sadistic element in Hitler's oratory. This was part of the drive for unrestricted power over other people, and in particular when they were in a crowd. In *Mein Kampf* Hitler had written of the speaker using his superiority to break the will of the audience.

As Stern noted, these elements in Hitler's speeches were not likely to impress liberal intellectuals, as opposed to the masses, but surely Hitler was not *interested* in impressing liberal intellectuals:

> What Hitler was offering . . . seemed to satisfy a whole spectrum of expectations and hopes – national, political, economic and social, cultural and even religious . . . He certainly appeared to believe in the State as a source of national cohesion and 'positive' politics. Only libertarians could have found nothing acceptable in his programme or in his promises; such men existed but they had no political following.
>
> (J. Stern, *Hitler – The Führer And The People*, Fontana, 1974, p. 103)

Hitler's speeches usually followed a pattern. They were delivered in the evening in order to create more atmosphere, an atmosphere in which the tension was enhanced by Hitler arriving late. Then the speech would begin. Hitler would recap some part of the party's history; there would be some threats and accusations, interspersed with snippets of information; the finish would include an emotional commitment by Hitler to maintain his resolve on behalf of his people.

Before every appearance, Hitler practised his speeches. He had them typed in large characters on a special machine, in order that he could read them without wearing spectacles. To do so, he thought, would not project the right image.

Hitler's speeches and appearances were often made to reinforce the commitment of the faithful. But they were also taken note of abroad. It was Hitler's intentions in foreign policy which increasingly concerned Europe's statesmen as the 1930s unfolded.

timeline	1933 January	Hitler appointed Chancellor
	February	Reichstag fire
	March	Reichstag elections: Nazis won 43.9 per cent of the vote
		Enabling Law passed
	April	Boycott of Jewish shops began
		The German states or *Länder* were co-ordinated
	May	Trade Unions banned

	July	Other political parties banned
		Concordat with the Catholic Church
	November	Reichstag elections and referendum. Nazis won 92 per cent of the vote
1934	June	Night of the Long Knives. Röhm and several political opponents murdered
	July	SS became an independent organisation within the Nazi Party
	August	Death of Hindenburg. Hitler nominated Führer. Approved by plebiscite
1935	March	Reintroduction of conscription
	September	Nuremberg Laws against the Jews. Reich Citizenship Laws
1936	August	Olympic Games in Berlin
	September	Announcement of Four-Year Plan
1938	February	Dismissal of the War Minister, von Blomberg, and the Commander-in-Chief, von Fritsch. Creation of High Command of the Armed Forces
	November	Kristallnacht. Attacks on Jewish property

Points to consider

1) To what extent had Hitler established Nazi control over Germany by the end of 1934?
2) What were the causes and results of the Röhm Purge?
3) How effectively did Hitler
   (a) govern Germany in the 1930s; and
   (b) manage the German economy?
4) In what ways, and why, have historians disagreed about Hitler's precise role in Germany in the 1930s?
5) How serious was Hitler's anti-Semitism, and how did it affect Nazi policy?
6) Was Hitler's lifestyle significant to his success as a leader?
7) Was Hitler a popular dictator? What were the reasons for his popularity?

HITLER AND FOREIGN POLICY

Whatever the arguments concerning Hitler's precise role in the internal affairs of Germany in the 1930s, there is no doubt that he was the prime mover in Germany's foreign policy. Nevertheless, there has been considerable disagreement among historians about Hitler's motivation and his exact plans. During the Second World War it had seemed quite clear, at least to the Allies: Hitler had pursued an aggressive foreign policy aimed at world domination, and was therefore entirely responsible for the conflict. Until 1938 commentators had been less sure: was Hitler bent on war, or simply trying to redress perceived wrongs inflicted on Germany in the peace settlement of 1919? Some years after 1945, revisionist historians confused the issue again by suggesting that Hitler was not *that* different from other statesmen, and that he had reacted to events as much as initiating action himself.

A GREATER GERMANY OR WORLD DOMINATION?

Hitler saw foreign policy as a combination of diplomacy and military policy. He felt equally confident in both spheres, just as he would have agreed with the old Clausewitz dictum that war is but an extension of politics by other means. One historian put it differently:

> Hitler ... regarded diplomacy as the continuation of the *struggle for power* inside Germany, and the years of experience, gained from street brawls, polemical warfare and mob oratory, had made up for his lack of professional training: indeed it had fitted him better for penetrating into the mind of his own

people and for winning mass support. That he could, with equal skill, so often apprehend and successfully exploit the weakness of foreigners, despite his notoriously absurd ideas about them and despite his tactical blunders, is frankly astonishing.

(E. M. Robertson, *Hitler's Pre-War Policy And Military Plans 1933–1939*, Longman, 1963, pp. 1–2)

Hitler was particularly skilful at appealing publicly to principles such as justice, when pressing German claims, because he knew that these principles were held to be important in the democracies.

He was clearly an expansionist. What is less clear is the precise nature of his expansionist aims. A related issue is whether Hitler actually intended war, or whether he simply accepted its possibility as a likely by-product of his territorial ambitions. Vague statements that imply that Hitler was simply power crazed and bent upon some non-specific 'world domination' are not very helpful to an assessment of his foreign policy. Interpretations which insist that Hitler pursued a precise programme or timetable in his foreign policy also raise problems for the historian. This despite the fact that Hitler wrote and said more than most politicians about his future intentions, during the early years of the Nazi movement.

A new German empire?

Hitler wrote at length in the 1920s about his territorial ambitions, and Germany's best course of action in foreign policy. The original Twenty-Five Point Programme of the party gave prominence to demands for an abrogation of the Treaty of Versailles, which had taken coveted areas of land from Germany; and called for the unification of all Germans in an empire or Reich. *Mein Kampf* also laid down the principles of foreign policy. The book contains the famous vision of a German empire being built in the East on the ruins of Communist Russia. Destiny pointed Germany towards Russia, as a means of acquiring living space for the German people, and because Russia, as the centre of Jewish Bolshevism, must be destroyed. Hitler was writing at a time when Weimar Germany was co-operating with Russia as a result of the Treaty of Rapallo, signed in 1922. He emphasised the danger of any sort of alliance with Russia. The Russian leaders simply could not be trusted. Moreover, only one continental power could exist in Europe. If that power were to be Germany, her people must prevent the emergence of a second great continental power, by force if necessary.

Lebensraum

There have been attempts to challenge the literalness of Hitler's ambition. Broszat dismissed *Lebensraum* (literally, 'living space') as an 'ideological metaphor', something proclaimed by the Nazis to help them overcome internal tensions by mobilising support for an expansionist policy which had no specific objectives. It is true that the Nazis developed no serious plans for resettling Russia. When they did occupy tracts of the country in 1941 they simply exploited the land for resources as any old colonial power, except that it was done in a particularly brutal fashion. However, denying the seriousness of Nazi ambitions or playing down the importance of ideology is dangerous: lack of serious planning was also evident in many other areas of Nazi activity besides *Lebensraum*, but we should probably be wary of belittling the importance of the ideological component.

The Second Book

In 1928 Hitler wrote the less well-known *Second Book* or *Secret Book*. In addition to repeating the message about German expansionism at the expense of Russia, this book also posed the possibility of a larger struggle between the United States and a German-dominated Europe. This was an extension of the theme first evident in *Mein Kampf*, that Germany would become a Continental power of world status. Above all, wrote Hitler in the 1920s, it was the function of foreign policy to secure the continued existence of the race. That, in turn, depended upon the acquisition of foreign territory. If possible, Italy and Britain should be enlisted as allies. France was an enemy, because she would not tolerate a German-dominated Europe. Hitler was critical of the foreign policies of the Weimar Republic, and before it the Imperial German Government, because among other faults, they had kowtowed to France and had been generally incompetent in protecting German interests.

Historians have argued at great length about the precise nature of Hitler's ambitions. This despite the fact that he wrote about his aims in advance. The debate has arisen partly because Hitler was not always so precise in his statements, and partly because the issue of Hitler's motives has become bound up with the long-term analysis of German ambition since the unification of the modern German State in 1871.

We can say with confidence that Hitler's early thoughts on foreign policy contained a mixture of traditional and revolutionary elements. The demand for a revision of the Treaty of Versailles had been voiced in the 1920s by other German politicians. The supposedly moderate Stresemann had sought a revision of the Treaty within the framework of international law and European consent. Brüning, von Papen and von Schleicher had been prepared for Germany to 'go it alone' in securing revisions, if necessary.

However, Hitler was to become noticeably more warlike in his approach. This is not to say that he was consistent. In 1919 his ideas were scarcely distinguishable from a number of pan-German agitators: the idea that Germany would have to resist Britain and France in order to overturn the Treaty of Versailles; the idea that Germany should receive back the colonies taken from her by the Treaty; and even the possibility of alliance with Russia, another power defeated in 1918. Hitler's views had changed by the time of *Mein Kampf* in favour of alliance with Britain, renouncing the return of colonies, and hostility to Russia. The changes came about partly because of the arguments of geopoliticians and partly becuse of the influence of the Nazi philosopher Rosenberg. Hitler did not admit to these influences, but they were undoubtedly at work. Despite these changes in emphasis, some of Hitler's earliest biographers, among them Bullock and Trevor-Roper, concluded that Hitler pursued the same aims in foreign policy from the early 1920s until well into the 1930s. This interpretation was typical of the 'intentionalist' school. This was at a time when Hitler's responsibility for causing the recently concluded war was already under debate.

The basis of German foreign policy

Some historians were anxious to look back even before the First World War to find the mainspring of German foreign policy. The work particularly of the German historian Fritz Fischer, who, in addition to investigating German ambitions before 1914, had highlighted the expansionist aims of the German Government and High Command during the First World War, aroused interest. This in itself sparked off a controversy: were those aims formulated only during the war itself, or were they actually partly responsible for Germany's aggressive behaviour on the international stage before 1914? Whatever the truth, the fact that some German politicians before 1918 had already professed expansionist aims apparently similar to those of Hitler, led the British historian A. J. P. Taylor to conclude in 1961 that Hitler was simply following in the footsteps of his predecessors.

One of the problems with this interpretation is that it tends to ignore the differences between Hitler's brand of nationalism and nineteenth-century nationalism. Hitler was novel among political leaders in identifying the nation with 'race'. He did not believe that it was possible to 'Germanise' other races. Such an attempt would result in a disastrous bastardising and degeneration of the German race. For Hitler, although he did not spell out this clearly in the early days, there was one obvious conclusion: expansionism could only mean the enslavement or extermination of other races rather than a fruitless attempt to accommodate them or absorb them. What is less clear is when he actually came to this conclusion. However, Taylor was to go much further in exciting controversy among fellow historians. Not content with putting Hitler alongside other supposedly more moderate German politicians of the past, Taylor went on in *The Origins of the Second World War* to query commonly held assumptions about Hitler's actions after 1933. He claimed that Hitler often acted opportunistically, in response to the actions of other powers. The German historian Mommsen also stressed the opportunistic nature of Hitler's responses to external pressures, governed partly by his desire to bolster his image with the German people. The battle lines were soon drawn. Was Hitler operating after 1933 on particular principles, or was he an out-and-out pragmatist? Was Hitler the prime mover in events? Do not the complexities of international affairs ensure that even a determined leader cannot always follow a blueprint? There are always other important actors on the international stage, and even dictators respond to internal pressures and concerns which might encourage or inhibit a radical foreign policy.

THE ROAD TO WAR?
—

Before examining some of these controversies at greater length, we should establish clearly how Hitler's direction of foreign policy unfolded after 1933. It is not disputed that Hitler was determined to destroy the territorial provisions of the Treaty of Versailles. Indeed, there were several on the right, particularly in Britain, who sympathised with Germany's sense of grievance. Hitler was to play skilfully on such emotions. However, he moved cautiously at first. The new Chancellor retained the Conservative von Neurath as his Foreign Minister, and tried to allay foreign apprehensions about German ambitions abroad while the Nazis consolidated their position at home. Although Hitler took Germany out of the Disarmament Conference and the League of Nations, it was done in such a way that Germany was presented as the injured party, suffering unfair treatment while established powers, particularly the French, refused to reduce the size of their army in line with the forced reduction in German forces. The Non-Aggression Pact signed with Poland in 1934 also enabled Hitler to pose as the leader offering an olive branch to the world. The reality of the pact was that it weakened Western influences in Poland. Hitler also took the plaudits when the German population of the Saar voted in 1935 to return to the Reich, 15 years after the Treaty of Versailles had placed the region under League of Nations' control.

Hitler was obliged to tread carefully. When Austrian Nazis attempted a coup in Vienna in July 1934, Mussolini successfully warned Germany off intervention. However, Mussolini was about to embark upon his own foreign adventures, which were eventually to distance him from the British and French and seduce him into the Axis Agreement with Hitler. Hitler himself felt secure enough in 1935 to challenge the Treaty of Versailles. He announced the existence of a German air force and the introduction of conscription. He combined this blatant challenge to the League Powers with protestations of his peaceful intentions. Agreeing to a surprise proposal by the British Government for a Naval Treaty also worked to Hitler's advantage. Permitting the Germans to increase the size of their Navy condoned Hitler's violation of Versailles, and drove a wedge between the British and French.

Remilitarisation of the Rhineland

In 1936 the British and French governments were preoccupied with the Italian invasion of Abyssinia, begun the previous year. Hitler seized the opportunity: brushing aside the hesitation of his nervous generals, Hitler ordered his troops into the demilitarised Rhineland. This had been a sensitive area for Germany. The Rhine–Ruhr region was important economically, and while demilitarised, there was always the possibility of a Western strike against Germany. That threat was now considerably lessened. It was a breach not only of Versailles, but also of the Treaty of Locarno, freely entered into by Germany in 1925. Had the French resisted, Hitler's orders were for the Germans to defend the banks of the Rhine. But the French would not act without the British. For good measure, Hitler also offered a non-aggression pact to the Western to reassure them of his good intentions. Verbal protests meant nothing. Germany had greatly increased her security in the West, and Hitler's prestige and his own confidence were greatly enhanced. His appetite was also whetted. When civil war broke out in Spain later in 1936, Hitler intervened on the side of Franco's Nationalists. It offered the prospect of future influence in the region plus the opportunity of practice for his forces. The Anti-Comintern Pact with Japan also signalled the rise in Germany's international confidence.

Invasion of Austria

Not all of Hitler's projects were successful. His ambassador von Ribbentrop failed in his mission to secure an agreement with the British. Germany was still not economically or militarily strong enough to risk a war. Therefore, 1937 was a relatively quiet year on the diplomatic front, but Hitler had already decided to move against his country of birth. By 1938 he could count on at least the quiescence of Mussolini. Powerful Nazi forces in Austria were causing disruption. The Austrian Chancellor Schuschnigg ordered a referendum to organise support. Hitler quickly ordered an invasion. It was unopposed. The Anschluss, or Union, of March 1938 destroyed Austrian independence. Austria became a province of the Reich.

Occupation of Czechoslovakia

Western inaction only fuelled Hitler's ambition. After the Anschluss, Czechoslovakia was partly surrounded by German territory. Although the Czechs possessed a large and well-equipped army, and strong natural defences, they were vulnerable. More than three million Sudeten Germans lived in the border regions. Although they had not been part of

Germany, there was agitation among them to join the Reich, an agitation fuelled from within Germany. France and the USSR had pacts with the Czechs, but the British attitude was crucial. All the indications were that the British Government wished for a peaceful settlement, and there was a willingness to believe that the Sudetenland would be Hitler's 'last territorial demand in Europe'. With a German invasion and war threatening in September 1938, the British Prime Minister Chamberlain twice flew out to Germany to deal with Hitler. Hitler stepped up his demands, and war seemed likely. But on Mussolini's initiative, a Four-Power Conference was arranged at Munich. Hitler was granted the Sudetenland, with all its strategic and material advantages.

Hitler guaranteed the remainder of the Czech State at Munich. But the following March he bullied the Czech President into allowing the break-up of the Czech State, much of it being annexed to Germany. It was a turning point. The excuse could no longer be used that Hitler was simply incorporating Germans in the Reich.

Poland

The British and French governments reluctantly faced the reality of Hitler's ambitions and guaranteed Poland, correctly perceived as Germany's next potential victim on her drive to the East. However, mutual suspicion between Britain and France on the one hand, and the USSR on the other, prevented these powers from making common cause against Hitler. Instead, Stalin saw an agreement with Hitler as a way of staving off a German threat and securing his own sphere of influence in central Europe, particularly since his negotiations with the suspicious and vacillating Western Governments were not bearing fruit. Hitler, by neutralising the USSR, could move against Poland in the expectation that without Soviet support, the British and French would probably not intervene to stop him. It may not have been an easy decision for Hitler to enter into the pact. He was temporarily relinquishing his territorial ambitions in the East, and a war against Britain and France would be a poor substitute if it materialised.

The Germans attacked Poland confidently in September 1939. When the British and French declared war on Germany two days later, Hitler was reportedly surprised. However, he appears to have given little thought to longer-term possibilities, such as American intervention. He would not be really content until June 1941, when, by invading the USSR, as one historian put it:

> ... he decided to adjust his military objectives to his final political aim. In so doing he violated the principle of limited liability to which he had owed his original success. From September 1939 he had on his hands a war which he could not win; from June 1941, a war he was certain to lose.
>
> (E. M. Robertson, *ibid*, p. 194)

DEBATING THE ISSUE

As stated earlier, it is beyond dispute that Hitler always intended to undo the Treaty of Versailles and to unite Germans in his Reich. It is also clear that he had territorial ambitions in Eastern Europe which went beyond this. However, the precise nature of any further ambitions, and the methods by which Hitler promoted his foreign policy, have long been debated. Was Hitler's empire to be continental, or some kind of 'world empire'? As described earlier, historians of the 1950s tended to

Hitler threatens the peace of Europe

focus on Hitler's eurocentric ambitions. But there were later dissenters. One of the exponents of the idea of Hitler as bent on world domination was the German historan Hillgruber, writing in 1963 (*Hitler's Strategie*). His evidence for this view included the developing interest which Hitler showed in a navy and colonies. This 'globalist' concept was taken up by Hildebrand and other historians. Their theme was as follows: Hitler's objective of world mastery was to be achieved by a *Stufenplan* or three-stage plan involving the establishment of German control first over the Continent, then over the British Empire, and finally over the United States. However, this was not taken to mean a precise timetable or complete consistency. Hildebrand accepted that Hitler's aims were not easily distinguishable from traditional revisionist demands for a long time, but he asserted that after the outbreak of the war in 1939, the more extreme ideas of racism and world domination increasingly came to the fore.

'Continentalists' like Trevor-Roper believed that Hitler's ambitions centred essentially on the enslavement of Eastern Europe. Historians of this persuasion knew of Hitler's late-night musings on innumerable subjects, which occasionally included the prospect of Germany dominating the world. However, they insisted that such musings could not be equated with an actual blueprint for action.

This was not the end of the debate. The fact that Hitler may or may not have had a long-term strategy of expansionism does not mean that his tactics were inflexible. It is possible for long-term goals and an opportunistic approach to be quite compatible, and indeed is often the hallmark of a successful politician. Bullock came round to this view in his interpretation of Hitler's foreign policy. Perhaps one reason for Mussolini's failure was that as a consummate opportunist, he appeared to have no clear-cut goals. A leader can combine opportunism with consistency in aims. However, the range of Hitler's ambitions may well have fluctuated with his moods and according to his audience at any particular time. It would be misleading always to look for consistency in thought as well as deed. It is also possible to be both fanatical and opportunistic in approach, although some historians have seemed unable to accept this. Charges of opportunism against Hitler were encouraged by the apparent contradictions and inconsistencies in Nazi actions – the pact with Poland in 1934 and an accommodation with Japan might be taken as examples – but there were solid reasons for

Hitler's actions at the time.

Undoubtedly Hitler's priority in 1933 was to break the shackles of Versailles, without provoking Britain and neighbouring states into action. He was assisted in this by an international situation which facilitated revision of the status quo. The United States was isolated and in recession. The USSR was preoccupied with agricultural and industrial transformation. Britain had concerns outside Europe, such as the Far East, where the Japanese were flexing their muscles. Italy was wary of German ambition, but was soon to become a revisionist power herself. The French were disunited and unlikely to act alone. All this was to Hitler's advantage, but he still displayed considerable skill in exploiting international situations. He understood, for example, the reluctance of many influential British people to consider fighting for the 1919 settlement, already discredited in the eyes of many. Hitler played on feelings of guilt about the Peace Treaty, and he also evoked sympathy for his anti-Communism. He continued to play a clever psychological game: sabre-rattling was quickly followed by the waving of olive branches. Annexations and breaches of Treaties could at first be presented as reasonable acts, and were accompanied by renunciations of further territorial claims. Early successes boosted Hitler's confidence. He began to believe that the Western powers would not seriously resist his ambitions in Central and Eastern Europe. Successes also reduced the likelihood of doubters inside Germany disrupting Hitler's progress.

It should be emphasised that Hitler was very much the driving force in determining German foreign policy, whatever his motives. Although several of the foreign policy initiatives of the early 1930s would have been on Stresemann's agenda in the previous decade, Hitler's personal stamp was very evident in later initiatives such as the remilitarisation of the Rhineland. It was even more true of events in 1938 and 1939. Hitler's activities in foreign policy make it very difficult to sustain an argument that he was a 'weak' dictator. When he *wanted* to act, he did so.

THE TAYLOR CONTROVERSY

The controversy over Hitler's aims and methods became most intense following the publication of A. J. P. Taylor's *The Origins Of The Second World War* in 1961. Taylor claimed to be simply looking at the evidence. His conclusions were plainly drawn: Hitler did not plan the Second

World War, a war which was not fought over great principles, as the victors came to believe in 1945. Taylor turned a number of accepted 'truths' on their head. He declared that Hitler was but an ordinary politician, one who in fact was less skilful in diplomacy than Neville Chamberlain. Hitler was a man who responded to events, and had no blueprint. He preferred to wait until opposing forces were weakened and confused, and then he acted. Hitler spoke only for effect. Evidence such as *Mein Kampf* was disdainfully dismissed as the stuff of all politicians, and not to be taken seriously. Taylor claimed that the sentiments of the book were coloured by the fact that it was written in the shadow of the French occupation of the Ruhr. The *Table Talk* comprised the dreams of a man who was trying to rationalise his conquests at the height of the Russian campaign. Hitler was never 'in control' of events, and in some celebrated instances such as the Anschluss, Hitler was as much taken by surprise by the events as anyone.

A typical German

Taylor's theories, skilfully argued as always, shocked many professional historians at the time. One of the many attacks on Taylor came from Trevor-Roper in *Encounter*. He criticised Taylor for painting Hitler as 'an ordinary German statesman', seeking only to restore Germany's 'natural' position in Europe.

Taylor was wrongly accused by some of 'whitewashing' Hitler. Taylor retorted that he was not assessing the morals of statesmen, but actually trying to show a line of continuity between Hitler and his forbears in Germany. Hitler might be different in temperament and even tactics from them, but essentially he was in the tradition of German politicians. The Germans had always sought to dominate Europe, particularly by controlling the East. Even Hitler's anti-Semitism was typically German. Taylor was also sympathetic to other politicians. If Hitler did not have plans, then it was difficult to blame other politicians for not stopping him. In that sense, none of the politicians were 'responsible' for the war. The only difference between dictators, like Hitler, and other statesmen was that 'their appetite was greater; and they fed it by more unscrupulous means'. But Hitler was only doing his best for his country, like most statesmen. He was certainly no more wicked than many others in principle, although he may have outdone others in deeds. 'In international affairs there was nothing wrong with Hitler except that he was a German.' Taylor was not trying to defend Hitler. He accepted that Hitler said and did some very nasty things, particularly inside Germany. In fact Taylor implied that other Germans were as bad as Hitler in going along with him. He explained brutal policies such as *Lebensraum* and all that that implied, by suggesting that these ideas were fuelled by the war *after* it had started, rather than the ideas bringing about war.

To some extent Taylor was only repeating the Fischer thesis that Hitler's aims were no more ambitious than those of the 1914–18 German politicians. But it was his style of argument as much as anything which aroused controversy. Taylor was accused of writing 'old-fashioned' history, by putting the diplomatic exchanges of politicians too much at the centre of events. He paid less attention to the economic and other pressures which influenced national policies. Taylor was also accused of being selective in his use of evidence, or contradictory. For example, having refused to take Hitler's writings seriously, Taylor says of Hitler: 'The unique quality in Hitler was the gift of translating commonplace thoughts into action ... The driving force in him was a terrifying literalism.' By treating Hitler as a 'rational' statesman, Taylor did not take his racist ideas seriously, and did not, therefore, understand Nazi policy towards the USSR. He certainly tried to explain the desire for *Lebensraum* in economic rather than ideological terms, and was not even convinced that Hitler planned for war against Russia.

Examining the evidence

Relying upon the evidence of Hitler's own writings and musings could be a dangerous technique, giving an unbalanced view. This is because the published records between 1933 and 1938 are rather sparse. Hitler did not keep a diary or write many letters. Many conversations were not recorded, particularly those with Nazis like Goebbels and Göring. Non-Nazis like von Neurath and von Bülow of the Foreign Ministry were more inclined to keep a record of conversations. When Hitler talked to a small and select audience, unofficial notes were sometimes taken: this is the origin of the famous Hossbach Memorandum, which will be considered later. But we must face the possibility that Hitler spoke very differently on different occasions to different audiences.

Occasionally, we do have a record of Hitler's ideas on foreign policy in the 1930s. At an early Cabinet meeting, on 8 February 1933, he declared that for the next four or five years, the main principle for Germany must be 'everything for the armed forces'. The next few years were spent rearming, although the perceptions of Hitler and his generals appear to have been different: they wished to use the army possibly to bargain a revision of the Treaty of Versailles in Germany's favour; Hitler was probably more ambitious. The remilitarisation of the Rhineland seems to have been a watershed. German sources themselves suggest that this was the last occasion when the Germans could have been stopped with relative ease. But Hitler had succeeded in his coup. From March 1936 onwards his strategy was more offensive. In August of that year he wrote a secret memorandum giving his views on the organisation of the German economy. It was unusual in being one of the few documents that he wrote himself as Chancellor. Hitler threatened in the document that he would follow the example of the Soviets in introducing a fully planned economy if the financiers and industrialists did not co-operate. The German economy and army must be ready for war in four years. After this document was written, responsibility for the Four-Year Plan was given to Göring rather than to the more conservative Schacht.

RELATIONS WITH BRITAIN

Hitler's relationship with Britain in the 1930s continued to be ambivalent. There were occasions when he expressed hopes of enlisting Britain as an ally. Hence von Ribbentrop's mission to Britain in 1936. But a year later Hitler declared that Britain was no different from France in wanting to prevent him from making territorial changes in Europe. Therefore, he declared his intention of building a battle fleet capable of challenging the Royal Navy, and this became a priority in 1939. It is difficult to find a consistent theme. His wish apparently was for Britain to allow him a free hand in dominating the Continent, while the British were secure in their overseas Empire. Hitler was apparently reluctant to take on Britain in an all-out conflict, not out of apprehension, but because he viewed such a prospect as unnecessary.

THE HOSSBACH MEMORANDUM

In November 1937 Hitler appeared to give real clues as to his ultimate aims. He held a secret meeting in the Chancellery. Hitler's comments were recorded by a Colonel Hossbach. The resulting document, which became known as the Hossbach Memorandum, was to be used at the Nuremberg War Trials as part of the evidence for Germany having planned aggressive war. However, in more recent years the document has aroused great controversy.

The Memorandum outlined Hitler's intention to acquire living space in Europe. He outlined possible scenarios, but declared that 1943–5 was the last chance for Germany to strike with time on her side. If the opportunity arose to act earlier against Austria or Czechoslovakia, he would seize it – if, for example, France was distracted by civil war.

The Hossbach Memorandum has been taken as evidence of a widening rift between the Führer and his generals. Hitler may have been testing his military leaders and Foreign Minister to discover the extent to which they would go along with him. Hitler appeared to be contemplating war, they wanted a postponement until Germany was much better placed. The fact that not long after this meeting, more moderate officers like Blomberg and Fritsch were replaced, along with Von Neurath in the Foreign Ministry, might lend support to this interpretation of Hitler's tactics. The changes were made following Hitler's last Cabinet meeting in February 1938. The German generals had based all their calculations on the balance of forces and concrete strategic factors. Hitler alone included psychological calculations in his balance sheet – and he rightly concluded that, whatever the state of their arms, the Western democracies were reluctant to fight. The Memorandum also represents a turning point in Hitler's views of Russia. Before this date he had insisted on the prime danger from Russia. He now revised his opinion: the Purges had weakened the Red Army, and it was less of an immediate threat. Therefore, Hitler said that after defeating Czechoslovakia, he would if necessary turn on the Western powers.

In another respect, the Hossbach Memorandum was not a turning point. No decisions followed, and moves against Austria a few months later were improvised.

A. J. P. Taylor thought that the Hossbach Memorandum was largely daydreaming or, at most, part of a domestic manoeuvre to win conservatives over to the idea of rearmament. The Memorandum contained no specific war plans, and assumed that if opportunities arose from which Germany could profit, they would arise from the actions of others. Taylor also claimed that the state of German armaments in 1939 was 'decisive proof' that Hitler was not intending a general war, and perhaps no war at all.

Taylor was probably correct in the latter statement: Hitler was thinking in terms of a Blitzkrieg or 'lightning war'. However, it is less easy to be dismissive of the Memorandum in all other respects. The reality is, the message of the Memorandum was quite compatible with the notion of Germany eventually creating an Empire, provided the right moment was recognised to move against potential enemies.

WAR ARRIVES

Had Hitler died in 1939, his foreign policy, whatever his successes domestically, would have marked him out as having been a successful leader. Whether he took the initiative in certain events or not, he had exploited them effectively in Germany's interests. By 1939 Germany was again militarily strong and the leading power in Europe. The pact with Stalin appeared to have averted the danger of a two-front war. Opposition within Germany to Hitler's foreign policy had been silenced. The German people as a whole did not want war, but they could not fail to be impressed by Hitler's success in restoring pride to Germany along with her Great Power status. But Hitler was not content to rest on his laurels. The invasion of Poland had been decided upon. It provoked a war with Britain and France, which Hitler may or may not have wanted in 1939. Some historians such as Werner Maser have accepted it as an indisputable fact that Hitler basically always wanted a war, although that does not, of course, mean that he wanted one in 1939. But now that it had arrived, Hitler put aside his initial doubts and threw himself enthusiastically into the struggle.

timeline	1933 September	Germany withdrew from the League of Nations and the Disarmament Conference
	1934 January	Non-Aggression Pact with Poland
	June	First meeting between Hitler and Mussolini
	1935 January	Plebiscite returned the Saar to Germany
	June	Anglo-German Naval Treaty
	1936 March	Remilitarisation of the Rhineland
	July	Start of German intervention in the Spanish Civil War
	October	Rome–Berlin Axis and Anti-Comintern Pact between Germany and Japan
	1937 November	The Hossbach Conference
	1938 February	Von Ribbentrop appointed Foreign Minister
	March	Anschluss with Austria
	September	Meetings with Chamberlain at Berchtesgarden and Godesberg Munich Agreement over Czechoslovakia
	October	German troops occupied the Sudetenland
	1939 March	German occupation of Czechoslovakia German occupation of Memel
	May	Pact of Steel between Germany and Italy
	August	Non-Aggression Pact between Germany and USSR
	September	German invasion of Poland

Points to consider

1) **What were Hitler's main objectives in foreign policy? Were they consistent?**
2) **To what extent had Hitler succeeded in fulfilling these objectives by 1939? How skilful were Hitler's tactics?**
3) **Why has the subject of Hitler's foreign policy aroused so much controversy?**
4) **To what extent was Hitler responsible for the Second World War?**

6

WARLORD

A TARNISHED REPUTATION

In September 1939 Hitler found himself as warleader as well as Chancellor of Germany. What was Hitler's role in the Second World War, and in particular, what was his contribution as a military strategist?

Hitler's reputation in the field of military strategy suffered for a long time from derogatory post-war analyses by his professional generals. One of the most able, von Manstein, wrote that Hitler not only exercised poor judgement in the political sphere, but also lacked military experience at the requisite level. His conduct of the war, wrote von Manstein, was characterised by 'his overestimation of the power of the will', leading to the substitution of 'brute force' for the art of war. Hitler's method of determining strategy meant doing away 'with the very essence of leadership'. (E. von Manstein, *Lost Victories*, Methuen, 1958, pp. 274–6, 280, 285)

Professional distaste for Hitler's war leadership is understandable, particularly since Hitler had repeatedly emphasised his own contempt for the German officer caste, and had undermined the independence of the Armed Forces even before the war had begun. But were the criticisms of the professionals justified?

Hitler had absorbed an astonishing amount of technical and military knowledge, and in so doing had impressed even seasoned observers. He was able to defend his position coherently in military discussions, and not just by bullying tactics, as has sometimes been claimed. Hitler frequently unnerved his staff by picking up the most minor inaccuracies in reports and catching out military 'experts' who were less well-

prepared than himself. He was less effective at cal[...]
assessing complex military situations. He was also sl[...]
possibilities of new weapons such as radar and jets.[...]
the latter was thereby retarded, in favour of the V[...]
far less military potential than the ground-to-air h[...]
have greatly enhanced German air defences later in the war. Hitler was
also reluctant to get involved in nuclear research.

Like many self-taught 'experts', Hitler's understanding only served
him up to a point, and there were limitations to his understanding of the
problems and potential of applied technology. Another of Hitler's faults,
according to William Carr, was his tendency to put too much faith in
quantity at the expense of quality. Halder, Chief of General Staff
between 1938 and 1942, claimed that Hitler paid too much attention to
the number of divisions in the front line. Carr concluded:

> . . . one is left with an overall impression of a man floundering
> in detail, a quartermaster with a touch of genius making heroic
> efforts to grapple with a whole range of problems beyond the
> capacity of one man to master.
>
> (W. Carr, *Hitler – A Study in Personality And Politics*,
> Edward Arnold, 1978, p. 82)

Grand strategy is the sphere of action in which political and major
military decisions overlap and intertwine. Hitler's direction of grand
strategy in the war could be faulted on several counts. He might even be
faulted for getting involved in war at all in 1939, especially since he faced
a potential conflict on two fronts, a repeat of 1914, for which the
Germans had been criticised at the time and later. However, having got
involved at all, Hitler's strategy for fighting the war had a certain logic.
He certainly remained true to his declaration of November 1939 that 'I
shall stand or fall in this struggle. I shall never survive the defeat of my
people. No capitulation to the outside forces, no revolution from the
interior forces.' (Conference with Supreme Commanders, 23 November
1939)

HITLER AND THE GENERALS

Hitler and Stalin conducted both strategy and foreign policy in their
respective countries. Often the demands of each sphere may conflict,

strains in the leadership. There were probably more tensions in German than the Soviet camp, although the tensions sometimes isted in Hitler's own mind. For example, Hitler sometimes forbade withdrawals which would have made sense on military grounds because he feared they might harm his reputation on the world stage. However, there were real strains in the headquarters where military strategy was hammered out, and this also helps to explain later criticisms of Hitler by the generals who survived him.

Hitler personally directed strategy through the High Command of the Armed Forces (OKW). This had been established in February 1938 under the subservient Keitel. Frequently OKW functioned as little more than a military secretariat, a rubber stamp for Hitler's 'inspirations'. Hitler made decisions, then his staff drew up operational plans to implement them. OKH, the High Command of the Army, was not well placed to argue with decisions, since it did not have a view of the whole. Keitel later used the fact that 'the OKW was merely the executive staff of the Supreme Commander' in his defence at the Nuremberg War Trials. Another General told the British military expert Liddell Hart

> The Polish, Western and Balkan campaigns were conducted by OKH – with comparatively little interference from OKW. The Battle of Kiev was the first occasion when Hitler attempted to take direct charge of operations . . . on the ground that it was essential to finish the Russian campaign before the winter. From then on, OKH was increasingly dominated by OKW – which really spelt Hitler.
>
> (B. Liddell Hart, *The Other Side Of The Hill*, Cassell, 1948, pp. 50–1)

The Commanders of the navy and air force had an advantage over the army in that they had more frequent access to Hitler, and he allowed them more latitude: Göring, because of his standing in the Party; and Admiral Raeder, as an enthusiastic Nazi supporter. Hitler's relationship with the army officer caste was far more ambivalent. General Beck was Hitler's Chief of Staff for five years, yet claimed that he was never given the opportunity to discuss his views on defence. This may have been a deliberate slight by Hitler. Hitler certainly distrusted professionals whose ability was not matched by enthusiasm. He did trust some generals and would occasionally listen to requests. For example, Hitler permitted von Runstedt to retreat to the Rhine in February 1945. But more often Hitler countered requests by his generals for permission to carry out specific manoeuvres with the blunt assertion that 'fanaticism' combined with the benevolence of Providence would ensure victory.

Hitler held audiences with the Commanders of the three Services separately. Such deliberate compartmentalisation in a structure which already encouraged specialisation, further strengthened Hitler's hand as the only man with an 'overall view' of the war.

There was nothing in Germany equivalent to the British War Cabinet. That might have allowed the opportunity for discussion which was anathema to Hitler. Yet isolating individuals, and particularly precluding co-ordination between the three Services, could have serious consequences. This was evident for example in the planning of Operation Sea Lion, the invasion of Britain: only in July 1940, when the Germans were just across the English Channel, did army leaders

WONDER HOW LONG THE HONEYMOON WILL LAST?

Wonder how long the honeymoon will last?,
Clifford Berryman, 9 October 1939

discover that their invasion plans were based upon an erroneous perception of the navy's capabilities, while there was no co-ordination with the Luftwaffe either.

Hitler's interference in military affairs increased when he made himself Commander-in-Chief of the army in December 1941. In 1942 he even assumed active command of an army group in Russia while 1,000 miles behind the front line.

THE AXIS

Lack of co-operation was not confined to internal affairs. It also percolated the sphere of grand strategy. Only sporadic consultations took place between Hitler and Mussolini. Their meetings were taken up with optimistic remarks on the course of the war and strategic developments in their broadest sense rather than concrete planning. Hitler did not even inform Mussolini about his invasion of Russia until it had begun. Relations with Japan were even more tenuous. Hitler simply hoped that fear of Japanese ambitions would deter the United States from becoming involved in a European war. There was no question of a combined Chiefs-of-Staff among the Axis Powers. From the start, Hitler

> did not want military help of any kind . . . Nor, frankly, would he care to share the victory with anyone . . . We Germans did not understand the methods of the British, who went about in the world begging in order to find nations that were willing to shed their blood for them and their aims.
> (Memorandum of Meeting between Ambassador Oshima and Hitler, 24 October 1939)

Yet, by the end of the war, Hitler was able to convince himself that his friendship for his allies, particularly Mussolini, was chiefly responsible for Germany's defeat!

THE *FÜHRER-PRINCIPLE* IN ACTION

Hitler was on stronger ground in his appreciation of psychology as an important part of strategy. It was an extension of his prewar skill of playing on the weakness of will among Western statesmen. His estimate of the importance of personality and will in war was part of his justification for the attack on Poland right at the beginning of the war:

> Probably no-one will ever again have the confidence of the whole German nation as I do . . . But I can be eliminated at any time by a criminal or an idiot.
> (Speech to his Commanders-in-Chief, 22 August 1939)

Hitler judged the possibilities for a successful attack in the West in 1940 more imaginatively than his more experienced generals. He gambled correctly. On the other hand, Hitler could make serious miscalculations. One such was his low estimation of the capacity of the Russians to resist an attack in 1941, although many others on both the Allied and Axis sides held similar views. Sometimes Hitler's famous 'intuition' was accurate: for example his belief by March 1944 that the Allies would invade Normandy, an intuition which his commander Runstedt ignored. His intuition could be off target, as was his belief that the Allies would invade Sardinia rather than Sicily. It could lead him into obsessions, such as that Norway was the decisive theatre of the war, a delusion which caused him to commit large numbers of German troops to its defence, when they were needed elsewhere.

German prospects were at their most precarious when Hitler indulged in his 'world historical perspectives'. These led to decisions of a general nature without adequate attention to any difficulties which might arise. The assumption was that 'Providence' would see him through. This explains the dry comment of the remarkable General Rommel that

> Excellent as our tactical achievements were in all theatres of war, there was not that solid strategic foundation which would have directed our tactical skill into the right channels.
> (Quoted in I. S. O. Playfair, *The Mediterranean And The Middle East*, Vol. III, HMSO, 1960, p. xix)

At the other extreme, as the war progressed Hitler often completely ignored the area of strategy for that of tactics, interfering in the smallest operations with little regard for the overall strategic situation. His interventions could be disastrous, as for example when he simply dismissed reports of enemy strength which he found unpalatable. There were few prepared to contradict him.

Hitler's Directives for the conduct of the war frequently reveal his defects as a strategist. Some were concerned with strategy in its broadest sense, laying down the guidelines for future operations: some dealt with operations during specific campaigns already in progress, and clashed with what the General Staff would have regarded as its prerogative. Some Directives gave the impression that war is a clockwork affair in which all the pieces would fall neatly into place. Some interfered with minor levels of command and must have caused confusion or resentment at the battle front.

Some historians have given Hitler more credit as a war leader. Alan Clark conceded that Hitler was at his least sure in the sphere of grand tactics, that is the level of handling corps or armies, but believed that he was capable on the one hand of planning campaigns, and on the other of conducting regimental actions (A. Clark, *Barbarossa*, Penguin, 1966). Many of Hitler's more pronounced flaws became prominent later in the war when it was already effectively lost. It should also be emphasised there were proven campaigners among Hitler's generals who did have the resolve to stand up to Hitler, sometime successfully, as even his critic Manstein acknowledged.

THE MONTHS OF TRIUMPH

Until June 1941 Hitler's approach to military operations was essentially 'indirect'. In attacking France and the Low Countries the Germans practised deep penetration behind enemy lines while avoiding direct assaults where possible. The Allies were kept guessing about Hitler's true objectives. Hitler may have hoped in September 1939 that France and Britain would not fulfil their obligations towards Poland, but when they did so, Hitler was clear about the way ahead. He refused to be perturbed by the much-vaunted French Army, and declared that Britain was the principal enemy. Britain possessed 'geopolitical security and protection by a strong sea power and valiant air force.' If the British would not make peace, Hitler felt that he had no alternative but to attack, since Germany was not in a position to rely solely upon economic warfare against Britain. The German war effort was geared to Blitzkrieg, or short, decisive campaigns. Serious naval expansion had only just begun, and the Luftwaffe was not designed for long-range strategic operations. Hitler's decision to use his army in the West while time was on Germany's side was understandable. He may be criticised for the unbalanced make-up of the Wehrmacht in 1939 – for strategic purposes it was essentially the army alone – but there were convincing arguments for using the forces at his disposal in the way that he did.

The invasion of France and the Low Countries was possibly Hitler's greatest military triumph. Hitler overcame the opposition of his more cautious generals, and indeed his own doubts and hesitations, which were later forgotten. Planned originally for October 1939, the operation was postponed 14 times until May 1940. Hitler had the foresight to agree to a variation on the old Schlieffen Plan of 1914. The German success in encircling the bulk of the Allied forces via the Ardennes was more decisive than the head-on clash in Belgium. OKH had been against an offensive in the West at all. Yet, in a few weeks, Hitler's forces stood

WHERE NEXT, MEIN FÜHRER?

Hitler ponders his next move as his victorious armies sweep through France
(cartoon by Low)

astride Western Europe, possibly only the error of not pushing home their advantage at Dunkirk preventing the complete destruction of the British forces also. Although Hitler had been less confident in carrying out the operation than in planning it, his success convinced him of his military genius. From that time onwards, he was to intervene more and more in tactical operations.

CONFRONTING BRITAIN

In the summer of 1940 Hitler savoured victory. Characteristically he humiliated the French by forcing them to capitulate in the very railway carriage in which the Germans had signed the Armistice of 1918. However, now that he had several alternatives open to him, Hitler was less decisive. No plans had been prepared for an invasion of Britain. He made protestations of goodwill towards the British, offering a settlement. David Irving claims that Hitler's 'maudlin, unrequited affection' for Britain was as genuine in the summer of 1940 as it had been a year earlier, and that is why he now pulled his punches, 'to the exasperation of his strategic advisers' (D. Irving, *Hitler's War*, Hodder and Stoughton, 1977, p. 82). This is overstating the truth. While Hitler may have had a sentimental admiration for the British aristocracy, those 'valuable specimens' as he referred to them, his reluctance to focus his attention on the destruction of Britain arose more from the fact that his mind was already turning Eastwards. He wanted a free hand in Russia. He was certainly loath to risk his army in an invasion of Britain without a guarantee of certain success. The failure of the Luftwaffe to destroy the RAF or to bomb the British into submission made such a guarantee a pipedream.

By the end of the war Hitler had persuaded himself that he had deliberately refrained from annihilating the British at Dunkirk in order to avoid 'creating an irreparable breach between the English and ourselves'. In reality the Directive for Operation Sea Lion was not issued until four weeks after the fall of France, because of the absence of prior planning. When the Directive was issued, it lacked conviction. It did not assume that an invasion would be absolutely necessary. Disagreements between the army and the navy over invasion plans, and the fact that Operation Eagle, the air offensive against Britain, was not co-ordinated with the military preparations for Sea Lion, highlighted the weakness of the German command system when Hitler himself was indecisive or lacked the conviction to carry a scheme through. The situation also mirrored the administrative confusion which existed in the Third Reich generally. Hitler was the man who had talked about the need for co-ordinated military planning, but was not prepared to disturb Göring's cherished independence as head of the Luftwaffe. Neither would Hitler devote enough resources to the navy, despite the threat which submarine warfare posed to Britain's lifelines.

Another avenue by which the Germans could weaken Britain's resistance was to attack her Empire and communications. Some commentators have condemned Hitler's reluctance to devote himself enthusiastically to a 'Mediterranean strategy'. For example, Carr claims that Hitler should have concentrated his efforts on Gibraltar, Malta and Suez, crushing the British lines of communication with her Empire. Carr accuses Hitler of holding an arrogant belief that if Germany were unchallenged on the Continent, Britain could never defeat her. Hitler was almost certainly correct, assuming that Britain had no major allies, a situation which existed only up to June 1941 when Hitler invaded Russia.

As it was, Hitler intervened in North Africa only when his Italian ally performed badly there. His continuing opinion that North Africa was a subsidiary theatre of war deprived Rommel of the forces with which such an able general might have inflicted considerably more damage upon the Allies than he did.

Although a direct invasion of Britain was not long on Hitler's agenda, there were other attempts to strike decisive blows in the drive for more victories. In 1940 and 1941 Hitler made several attempts to bring Spain into the war in order to capture Gibraltar and seal off the Mediterranean. He was disappointed in his attempts to win over Franco. He made an unfavourable comparison between arguing with the Spanish dictator and a visit to the dentist.

It cannot be claimed with any conviction that a successful 'Mediterranean strategy' would have forced Britain to sue for peace. The Mediterranean was less vital to Britain's strategic position than the sea lanes of the Atlantic. The German U-boats inflicted great damage on British shipping there, but Hitler had not devoted enough resources to the German navy to make its successes decisive.

BARBAROSSA

Hitler's real objective, almost an obsession, was Russia. From the summer of 1940 Hitler regarded theatres such as the Balkans and North Africa not as integral to his strategy, but as areas of operations designed to protect Germany's flanks or to aid his hapless ally Mussolini. Having failed to induce the Spanish, the Vichy French, the Japanese and the Italians to do just as he wished – essentially diplomatic failures – it was with some relief that Hitler turned to preparations for Barbarossa, the campaign to destroy Soviet Russia and win living space in the East. A successful campaign there would fulfil ideological objectives – the destruction of the fount of Communism – and it would provide resources and land for German settlers. It would also make Germany so powerful that not only would Britain have no hope left of victory, but even the United States would be more reluctant to become involved in Europe. Hitler was anxious to use his army, which had been blooded successfully and was at its peak of confidence. According to General Halder, the decision to attack Russia 'came anything but easily to Hitler'. But on the eve of the invasion Hitler told Mussolini that he felt 'spiritually free' again, now that the die was cast.

With the benefit of hindsight, the decision by Hitler to attack Russia might be criticised on many grounds: political, economic and moral among them. At the time there were conflicting pressures. Hitler had not conquered Britain, although admittedly the British were not in any condition to threaten German supremacy on the Continent. Hitler had often condemned two-front wars. On the other hand, Russia's military potential was growing, and this influenced Hitler's decision to resolve Germany's 'problem of space' at the latest by 1943–5. His military intelligence service did not give him accurate information, as indeed it served him quite poorly throughout the war. However, there was clear evidence of how badly the Soviet Army had performed in its recent war against Finland, and it would take time for hurried Soviet military reforms to take effect. If Germany were to attack Russia, the time seemed right. The Allied intelligence services must have implicitly agreed, since they predicted that the Soviet Army would collapse within six weeks of a German invasion.

Hitler's initial precept was to destroy as much of the Soviet forces as possible in the shortest available time. This was a sounder strategy than one of gaining superficial kudos from simply acquiring large tracts of territory. Hitler's initial resolve that only 'a surprisingly rapid collapse of Russian resistance' could justify simultaneous efforts to capture the great cities of Moscow and Leningrad, was also sound.

The invasion began promisingly for the Germans. However, developing Soviet resistance forced Hitler to review his strategy as the summer of 1941 wore on and the enemy remained in being, despite enormous losses. While a drive towards Leningrad in the North and one towards the South continued, the Moscow Army Group Centre was put on the defensive. Some critics have condemned this as a military error, believing that an early and concentrated assault on Moscow would have been successful and would have brought the war to an end. Moscow was important as an industrial and communications centre, and as a political symbol. However, the enthusiastic German generals underestimated the potential dangers of a rapid and exposed tank thrust towards Moscow, and it is unlikely in any case that the fall of Moscow alone would have ended the war. Hitler, however, might be criticised for his decision to attack Moscow later in the year. Even then when his troops came to a standstill in the Russian winter, and the Soviets counter-attacked, Hitler's order to his army to stand firm probably prevented a setback for the Germans from becoming a rout.

A CHANGE IN FORTUNE

In the spring of 1942 Hitler reviewed his strategy. In December 1941, following the Japanese attack upon Pearl Harbor, Hitler had already taken the momentous step of declaring war upon the United States. But his principal concern was still Russia. In 1942 he decided to concentrate the German thrust in the South. As the offensive progressed, Hitler split it into two directions, towards the Caucasus and Stalingrad, although neither objective was essential to the other. Hitler became obsessed with Stalingrad, the city bearing his rival's name, and he allowed the large Sixth Army to become bogged down in the city as the Soviets moved in for the kill. Hitler obstinately refused to allow his troops to withdraw. Eventually the remnants of the army surrendered, and the Germans had suffered their biggest single defeat thus far in the war.

SO YOU DIDN'T KEEP MY PROMISE! YOU'RE FIRED!

British cartoonist Low's comment on Hitler's failure at Stalingrad

THE AILING FÜHRER

The change in Germany's military fortunes was paralleled by a deterioration in Hitler's health. During 1941 he began to complain of fainting fits, shivering and nausea. During 1942 and 1943 visitors to Hitler's headquarters commented on his more elderly appearance, and the fact that he walked with a stoop. He was also more excitable. Mentally he appeared more unstable: increasingly he veered between making snap decisions and not making up his mind at all. One post-war theory was that Hitler was suffering from the onset of Parkinson's disease, another that he was exhibiting the effects of Morell's drugs. However, Hitler maintained that the drugs, which Morell himself claimed contained mainly dietary supplements, actually improved his health. By 1944 Hitler was suffering from jaundice. In July of that year a group of conspirators, comprising disaffected army officers and other conservative opponents of Hitler, carried out an attempt to blow up Hitler at his headquarters, and hopefully shorten the war. Hitler survived the explosion. However, by 1945 he was in a state of near physical collapse, as was recorded in the report of a staff officer in the spring of that year:

> Physically he was a frightful picture. He dragged himself along slowly and painfully from his living quarters to the conference room in the bunker, the upper part of his body thrust forward, his legs drawn along behind. He had lost his sense of balance . . . His eyes were bloodshot . . . Saliva often dropped from the corners of his mouth – a horrible and pathetic sight.

The change in Hitler after 1942 had important effects on the conduct of the war, as a German historian graphically described:

> Hitler's illnesses were neither transitory nor imaginary; they were permanent factors which exerted an increasingly negative influence. At the end of 1942 his inspiration in the field of strategy left him, never to return, nor was there any consistent military planning after this time. Thenceforward he shunned risky undertakings and, in the conduct of operations, would permit no flexibility where long-term objectives were concerned. He never voluntarily surrendered conquered territory, as circumstances after 1943 sometimes demanded, and he refused to weaken secondary fronts and theatres of war in favour of more crucial ones. Moreover he postponed unpleasant decisions for as long as possible, even when a rapid decision was called for . . . he had become an overcautious, obstinate, intransigent old man.
>
> (Werner Maser, *Hitler*, Allen Lane, 1973, p. 303)

This is a more accurate picture than Hitler's own in 1944, one which was characterised by self-delusion:

> My task, especially since the year 1941, has been never to lose my nerve under any circumstances, but rather, if there is a collapse somewhere, always to find solutions and expedients in order to set things moving again.

INSIDE THE 'WOLF'S LAIR'

Hitler led an almost reclusive existence for much of the war. His headquarters in 1939 were first established in a special train in Poland; then near the west German frontier; and then in July 1941 he moved to the east. Apart from a brief period in the Ukraine he spent the next three years at his 'Wolf's Lair' headquarters at Rastenburg in East Prussia. It was here that the 1944 bomb plot almost succeeded. In this remote headquarters Hitler indulged in his wide-ranging monologues at meal-times at the end of the day. They were recorded and edited by Bormann, with Hitler's approval, and handed down to posterity as *Hitler's Table Talk*. After the depressing news of Stalingrad in the autumn of 1942, Hitler's audience was limited: no more officers, but principally his secretaries, his immediate staff and doctor. There was less mention of the war, and Hitler was more inclined to speak about his early years. There were still occasional visits to the Berghof, but mostly contact with the outside world was very limited. This was the principal reason why Bormann·became increasingly influential in controlling access to Hitler. Even Eva Braun was not admitted to the 'Wolf's Lair'; the only women allowed were Hitler's secretaries and a cook.

FIGHTING TO THE END

After Stalingrad the economy was finally put on a proper war footing, and Goebbels preached 'Total War'. It was to no real avail. The strategic initiative was effectively with the Allies. Hitler had no illusions about the prospects of a political settlement – he commented that such notions were 'childish and naive' unless a nation was enjoying successes rather than defeats – and there is no convincing evidence that he ever sought one.

Hitler's strategy in the second half of the war was principally that of static defence. He put considerable faith in fortifications in the West – such as the unfinished Atlantic Wall – and permitted withdrawals in the East rarely and reluctantly. He forgot the dictum of his hero Frederick the Great that 'He who would defend everything defends nothing at all'.

This strategy was certainly wasteful of life and resources. However, it is difficult to agree with critics like Manstein who argued that a strategy of mobile operational defence would have offered more prospects of success. Localised successes could not turn the tide against a coalition of increasingly overwhelming resources, and one which was determined on Germany's unconditional surrender. Hitler's faith in 'miracle weapons' or a split in the Allied coalition was naive, but he may have realised in his heart that the war was lost by 1943. General Jodl certainly claimed that Hitler knew that victory was impossible after the winter of 1941–2, although Hitler continued to pontificate on what the post-war world would be like after a German victory. Hitler still insisted that victory would be achieved one way or another – *so oder so* was one of his favourite expressions. The tide had effectively turned by the end of 1941: Hitler had failed to defeat Russia in a Blitzkrieg and, thenceforward, faced the massive war economies of the Soviets and the Americans. But realistically it would have been impossible for Hitler to have changed course suddenly in 1942 and 1943 and to have worked for a compromise peace. The anti-Hitler conspirators in Germany knew this, which was precisely why they plotted to eliminate him.

DEATH IN BERLIN

The collapse of his Italian ally, the relentless advance of the Red Army from the East, the successful invasion of Normandy by Allied forces in 1944, constant bombing of the Reich from the air – Hitler's defeat could only be a matter of time. The V weapons arrived too late. Desperate hopes of cracks in the Allied coalition were dashed. As the Red Army closed on Berlin, Hitler determined on a last stand in Bavaria. Then he changed his mind. Cooped up in his Berlin bunker, he issued impractical orders and exacted revenge on those Nazis who sought to escape the tightening net. He appears to have finally decided upon suicide on hearing of Himmler's defection. Hitler married the faithful Eva Braun, arranged their suicide, and ordered their bodies to be burned afterwards, lest they fall into Soviet hands. Despite much lurid speculation since, there is no convincing evidence that Hitler 'survived' or 'escaped'.

Hitler's obstinacy in prolonging the war added to the immense suffering in Europe. But right to the end he would accept no responsibility for Germany's defeat. He declared shortly before his own death, in April 1945, that 'If the German people loses the war, it will have proved itself not worthy of me'. Such contempt was harsh particularly on those non-Nazis among the Germans who had fought courageously for their country. But having got Germany into war in 1939, and having greatly extended the war in 1941, Hitler used the German Army more effectively than his critics sometimes allowed. A key moment in the war was the summer of 1940. Having no immediate plans for the invasion of Britain, Hitler was hesitant about relying on a war of attrition. Having then taken the plunge of attacking Russia, he failed to defeat Stalin in 1941. The failure of the Blitzkrieg meant that the war was effectively lost, since Germany was committed to a long conflict for which she was not adequately prepared. The nails were not driven into the German coffin for three more years, since the Germans resisted stubbornly. When it was all over, some German generals were anxious to disassociate themselves from Hitler, or to prove that they could have performed much better without him. Like Hitler himself, many of them failed to appreciate the enormity of the challenge of taking on and fighting total war in the modern age against two countries – the USA and USSR – whose resources as developing superpowers were already shifting the centre of world power away from central Europe, a process merely hastened by the war.

timeline	1939 September	German invasion of Poland
		Britain and France declared war on Germany
	November	Assassination attempt on Hitler in Munich
	1940 April	German invasion of Denmark and Norway
	May	German invasion of Netherlands, Belgium, Luxembourg and France
	June	French signed Armistice
	1941 April	German invasion of Yugoslavia and Greece
	June	German invasion of USSR
	December	German declaration of war on USA
		Hitler appointed himself Commander-in-Chief of the army
	1942 January	Wannsee Conference arranged for the 'Final Solution'
	November	German defeat at El Alamein
		Allied landings in North Africa
	1943 January	German surrender at Stalingrad
	February	German declaration of 'Total War'
	May	German surrender in North Africa

July	Allied landings in Sicily and overthrow of Mussolini
1944 June	Allied landings in Normandy
July	Bomb plot against Hitler
1945 January	Hitler's last broadcast
April	Hitler's marriage to Eva Braun and suicide
May	Unconditional surrender of Germany

Points to consider

1) **To what extent did Hitler determine Germany's military strategy during the war?**
2) **Did Hitler's strategy and tactics change during the course of the war?**
3) **What were Hitler's strengths and weaknesses as a war leader? Why has there been so much criticism of his war leadership?**
4) **To what extent was Hitler responsible for Germany losing the war?**

7

HITLER AND THE HISTORIANS

GERMANY'S FATE OR GERMANY'S MISFORTUNE?

It is not the purpose of this book to explain and interpret Nazism as an historical phenomenon. That would be a difficult task given the amount of literature produced since 1945, and even earlier, and the problem of analysing an era which, in the opinion of some commentators, defies rational analysis. There have been attempts by German historians to come to terms with the past of their own country. Non-Germans have been even more eager to do so. Was Nazism an aberration or in important respects simply a continuation of trends already present in German history?

The purpose of this chapter is more modest. It is to examine interpretations of Hitler both as a personality and as a political leader. Although a more limited aim, it is a worthy one. Only an examination of Hitler as a person can help to explain his rise to power ahead of so many superficially more credible contemporaries, including several rival right-wing would-be dictators. Presenting Hitler as a demon does not do the subject justice – after all he did have human qualities, including several unattractive ones – and our task should be, therefore, to make him more intelligible as a human being. Then we are in a better position to investigate why so many Germans in the 1920s and 1930s responded so positively to this human being. But Hitler was also much more than just an interesting personality. He was alive at a time when Germany was undergoing dramatic and traumatic changes. Hitler was as much a product of these events as he was an influence on later events himself. Therefore, the student of History studies both the personality and the events. When the two combine or overlap, profound issues come to the forefront. One such is this: was Hitler Germany's fate, the product of trends present in German history since the unification of the State under Bismarck? Or was he simply Germany's misfortune, an aberration in the history of a country which was new but in the mainstream of European civilisation, until the perverted philosophies of Nazism attempted to create a 'New Order', both in Germany and thoughout Europe?

EARLY INTERPRETATIONS

At the time of Hitler's rise to prominence, he was simply not understood by many observers. In an article in the *Daily Express*, the British Prime Minister Lloyd George went so far as to describe Hitler as 'the George Washington of Germany – the man who won for his country independence from all her oppressors'.

Early analyses of Nazi Germany tended to focus on Hitler, although they also considered the nature of his dictatorship. Important biographies of Hitler appeared as early as 1935. Rudolf Olden and Konrad Heiden were the authors. Disagreements about Hitler were current even before and during the war. Allied propaganda veered between depicting him as a Chaplinesque clown and a figure of pure evil. In contrast, sympathisers preferred to see him as a man of peace, seeking only fair treatment for Germany.

Two eminent British historians, Hugh Trevor-Roper and Alan Bullock, entered the field soon after the war. The former published *The Last Days Of Hitler* in 1946, and the latter *Hitler: A Study In Tyranny* in 1952. These were authoritative works, very influential, and in some respects still not completely surpassed.

Trevor-Roper's view

Both Trevor-Roper and Bullock put the Führer at the very centre of events, so much so that it would be difficult for a student relying solely upon their interpretations to conceive of any type of Fascist Germany had there been no Hitler. Trevor-Roper in a later book described Hitler's mind as 'coarse, turbid, narrow, rigid, cruel. It had nothing to recommend it but its power; and mental power, though important, is not by itself attractive'. (*Hitler's Table Talk* p. ix) Yet, for Trevor-Roper, it was a fascinating subject. He took the view that Hitler's ideas were crystallised in Landsberg Prison, while formulating *Mein Kampf*, and were fixed from thence onwards. This constancy of ideas meant a mind 'infinitely squalid in its miscellaneous cumber – like some huge barbarian monolith, the expression of giant strength and savage genius, surrounded by a festering heap of refuse.' He concluded that Hitler was one of the 'terrible simplifiers' of history, 'the most systematic, the most historical, the most philosophical, and yet the coarsest, cruellest, least magnanimous conquerer the world has ever known.' (*ibid.* p. xxxv)

The interest in Hitler was understandable, although he was a sensitive subject. Opinion polls carried out in West Germany in 1953 suggested that 32 per cent of the population thought that Hitler had been an outstanding leader, apart from making a few 'mistakes'. In 1958 15 per cent of Germans surveyed claimed they would be willing to vote for someone like Hitler, and more Germans disapproved rather than approved of the opposition towards Hitler that had existed in Nazi Germany. Only when West Germans felt more prosperous and secure in the 1960s did admiration for Hitler become restricted to extreme neo-Nazi groups. But the interest in him remained.

Bullock's view

Bullock's magisterial biography was first published in 1952 and is deservedly still read. Powerful and influential as the biography is, it has been criticised for a one-dimensional approach which failed to convey a real understanding of the man behind the dictator's mask. Many more revealing studies have appeared since 1952, but criticisms of Bullock's work are perhaps unjust, given that it was a pioneering study. Bullock did attempt to put Hitler into an historical context, although clearly presenting him as the leader who largely dictated events, a man who was very much master in his own house. Paradoxically, although Hitler was at the centre of Bullock's writing, he claimed that Hitler's personality shed little light on his historical importance.

Bullock thought that Hitler's career benefited from a share of luck and the disunity of his opponents, but he conceded that he also had abilities: 'his mastery of the irrational factors in politics, his insight into the weaknesses of his opponents, his gift for simplification, his sense of timing, his willingness to take risks.' (*Hitler: A Study In Tyranny* p. 804) These powers were combined with 'an ugly and strident egotism, a moral and intellectual cretinism . . . his twelve years' dictatorship was barren of all ideas save one – the further extension of his own power and that of the nation with which he had identified himself . . . The sole theme of the Nazi revolution was domination, dressed up as the doctrine of race, and, failing that, a vindictive destructiveness . . .' (*ibid.* p. 804)

Bullock regarded Hitler as being Germany's fate rather than her misfortune, identifying certain features in German history that favoured the rise of a radical right-wing movement: the traditions of nationalism, militarism, authoritarianism and the exaltation of the State, among others. But Bullock also regarded Hitler as representative of a more general European rejection of liberalism, simply taken to extremes in Germany.

A much later study by Bullock, *Hitler And Stalin – Parallel Lives*, published in 1991, did not add much to the debate. It did identify some of the more recent controversies, for example whether Hitler had been a 'weak' dictator, but the author did not pursue them in depth. He did, however, reach a new conclusion about Hitler's ultimate failure. It was that he fell victim to his own myth:

> No-one took the Hitler myth more seriously than Hitler himself, both the manipulation and the response . . . But success was fatal. When half Europe lay at his feet, Hitler abandoned himself to megalomania and became convinced of his own infallibility. But when he began to look to the image he had created to work miracles of its own accord – instead of exploiting it – his gifts deteriorated and his intuition played him false . . . Hitler played out his 'world-historical' role to the bitter end. But it was this same belief which curtained him in illusion and blinded him to what was actually happening, leading him to commit the sin which the Greeks called *hybris*, of believing himself to be more than man. No man was ever more surely destroyed by the image he created than Adolf Hitler.
>
> (A. Bullock, *Hitler And Stalin – Parallel Lives*,
> HarperCollins, 1991)

GERMANS COME TO TERMS WITH HITLER

Some interpreters found it difficult to distinguish between Hitler and other Germans, perhaps a legacy of wartime fear of the enemy. This sentiment lingered on even in the popular work of William Shirer, *The Rise And Fall Of The Third Reich*, published in 1960. Shirer had been in Berlin in the 1930s. His experience had not lent him perspective. He went so far as to claim that Germans as far apart as Luther and Nietzsche had been in some respects forerunners of Hitler.

Serious British and American historians sometimes focused upon Hitler's personality because they felt on safer ground than trying to interpret German history, about which they knew less. Perhaps for this reason also they often credited Hitler with more original ideas than did German historians, who were steeped in the history of their own country. Nevertheless, Germans themselves often approached their subject from different standpoints. Back in 1936 Konrad Heiden had raised the issue of the extent to which Hitler's actions were premeditated. He concluded that, while exhibiting opportunism, 'All Hitler's truly political acts derive from the programme set out in *Mein Kampf*'. (K. Heiden, *Adolf Hitler*, Zurich, 1936, Vol. 2, p. 259)

In complete contrast, Franz Neumann in *Behemoth*, published in 1944, made little mention of Hitler at all. He argued that Nazism represented 'totalitarian monopoly capitalism', with the Nazi state resting on the pillars of the bureaucracy, industry, and the expanding party and army. This was a version of the Marxist argument that Hitler was but a shadowy puppet of monopoly capitalism, determinedly destroying German democracy and preparing for aggressive war in order to maximise power and profits. Variations on this basic theme were to be peddled mostly, but not exclusively, in the Communist Eastern bloc for years to come. In contrast, some non-Marxist historians in the West were keen to examine the concept of totalitarianism and to stress the similarities between Nazism and Soviet Communism. They identified some qualities common to both Hitler and Stalin, while conceding that Hitler had certain unique characteristics.

J Stern, in *Hitler – The Führer And The People*, published in 1975, preferred to discount theories of manipulation or paranoia. He argued that for 25 years, until 1944, Hitler was capable of 'entirely rational and realistic views', which were not untypical, but simply pushed to a stronger and more uncompromising turn than usual in political leaders. Stern went on to rather spoil his argument about typicality by focusing on Hitler's 'destructive passion', which found fulfilment in the Russian campaign. Hitler was lured by 'the prospect of universal annihilation which included his enemies, his victim, his people and himself'. Stern concluded that 'Not conquest but indiscriminate annihilation was his aim.' (p. 221) Such obsessions are hopefully not typical of most politicians.

Revisionist interpretations of Hitler's role in Germany had already gained currency in that country in the 1960s. Mommsen, in *Civil Servants In The Third Reich* (1961) and Broszat, in *The Hitler State* (1969), pursued the so-called functionalist argument. Hitler was depicted as aloof from domestic affairs and power struggles carried on by underlings. These historians saw Hitler's role as holding together antagonistic forces which might otherwise have destroyed Germany from within. There was no conception, unlike in the works of Trevor-Roper or Bullock, of a man of consistent goals. Rather, according to Mommsen, Hitler was 'a man of improvisation, experimentation and of sudden impulses'.

Hildebrand emphasised that Hitler must be distinguished from National Socialism as such, but recognised the importance of Hitler's personality in any interpretation of events: Nazism could never have become the driving force in Germany without him. Hildebrand did accept that Hitler's Nazism, a combination of the traditional and the revolutionary, had elements of continuity with German history, but he asserted that its blatant racism marked it out as a movement apart. This is a reasoned analysis, although by itself it does not explain why so many Germans accepted Hitler in the early 1930s.

THE PSYCHO-HISTORICAL APPROACH
—

There remained historians who regarded Hitler's role in Germany as all-important, even if they could not agree about the precise nature of that role. The 1970s witnessed a spate of books which focused on Hitler, but in a very different way from the Bullock or Trevor-Roper approach. These were the 'psycho-histories'. Psycho-historians studied Hitler's personality in great detail, and paid particular attention to his early life as a means of explaining his motivation and later behaviour. There was intense speculation about Hitler's relationship with his mother. She, partly through a need to compensate for her 'guilt' at the deaths of her first three children, had a deep and unhealthy relationship with the infant Adolf. She was very protective of him, but also expected him to make a name of himself in the outside world, and this supposedly created feelings of extreme tension and insecurity in the young boy. The American psychologist Erich Fromm in *Escape From Freedom* (1941) had already investigated Hitler's 'defensive mechanism' whereby he always claimed to be defending himself when sadistically ill-treating others, and accused his enemies of having his own objectives. A later more extreme theory was put forward by Rudolf Binion in *Hitler Among The Germans*: 'Klara's overprotective nature and excessive feeding of her infant son stimulated an anxious quest for food and security which was responsible for Hitler's adult obsessions with Lebensraum.'

One of the more credible 'psycho-histories' was Robert Waite's *The Psychopathic God – Adolf Hitler*, published in 1977. Waite made great play with Hitler's many neuroses and closely examined his physical and mental characteristics: his obsession with memories of childhood and his continued liking for 'childish' things like sweets and circuses; his enthusiasm for practical jokes which humiliated other people; his concerns about sin and guilt which he projected on to the German nation; his fascination with death (Waite points out that the Nazis were at their best when staging death celebrations), blood, syphilis and wolves. Waite also brought out the contradictions: here was a man who regarded himself as honest and direct, but also a man who was an expert at dissimulation and at fooling people; a pragmatist who lived in a fantasy world; a man who had exhibited great bravery, but who was frightened by germs, water, moonlight and horses; a man who was prudish but relished pornography. In short, 'Hitler was both a pathetic little man filled with self-pity and an awesomely effective dictator.' For all Hitler's peculiarities, Waite was impressed by the public persona: 'Like all really great political leaders, he combined political realism with unshakeable belief in his historic destiny.' (R. Waite, *The Psychopathic God – Adolf Hitler*, Basic Books, 1977, pp. 42 & 44)

Waite claimed that most of Hitler's childhood characteristics simply became more pronounced in later life, and therefore were crucial to an understanding of the man. Certainly such analyses can be useful in contributing to the overall picture. However, there can be a problem with the psycho-historical approach, as summarised by William Carr, who wrote one of the better biographies of Hitler:

> In theory an alluring blend of historical insight and psycho-analytical experience, in practice, however, works classed as psycho-historical turn out all too often to be written by psychiatrists without any historical training or by historians primed with psycho-historical jargon.
>
> (W. Carr, 'The Hitler Image In The Last Half-Century', in
> H. Koch, *Apsects Of The Third Reich*, Macmillan, 1985, p. 473)

All human beings probably have fixations, some perhaps more than others, but focusing on an individual does not necessarily explain *how* the resulting tensions are translated into political action, partly because they do not satisfactorily explain the *context* in which that individual and his society exist. If Hitler became a politician because he failed as an artist, as he claimed in his *Table Talk*, why did all the other failed artists in Germany not become equally notorious? Only an examination of the wider context can allow a meaningful analysis of complex political situations.

OTHER MAJOR BIOGRAPHIES

The respected German historian Karl Bracher, in contrast to the psycho-historians and earlier biographers, had no time for Hitler as a personality. Bracher found Hitler uninteresting as a person, and regarded the history of his *movement* as far more significant than Hitler himself. Bracher was typical of many contemporary historians who have researched aspects of Nazi history, sometimes in a local and very detailed context. They have uncovered interesting information about the attitudes of ordinary people, but have deliberately shied away from an emphasis on famous personalities. This 'History from below' has been a valuable contribution to our understanding of Nazi Germany. However, some historians have continued to see a value in studying the key players on the political stage. Some biographies of the 1970s were 'traditional' in approach. Werner Maser in *Hitler* (1971) and Joachim Fest in his book of the same title (1973) researched some new areas, but added little to earlier works like that of Bullock. Maser did, however, carry out useful research into Hitler's years in Vienna, and was able, for example, to rebut firmly Hitler's claims to youthful poverty. Fest labelled Hitler as an 'unperson' and a 'neurotic character', but did not convincingly explore the possible implications of these labels.

John Toland in *Adolf Hitler* (1976) and Norman Stone in *Adolf Hitler* (1980) emphasised Hitler's importance, but added little to the debate. William Carr in *Hitler – A Study In Personality And Politics* (1978) did attempt a different approach. Carr was concerned that 'traditional' biographies of important figures in the complex modern world did not take enough account of the pressures under which rulers and the ruled lived. Carr believed that 'great men' influence events in different ways and at different times. As an example, Carr considered Hitler and the Holocaust. He pointed out that 'traditionalists' like Bullock and Maser saw the Holocaust as a logical extension of Hitler's long-held racist views. Some revisionists, notably Irving, argued that Himmler was responsible and kept Hitler in the dark until 1943. Carr suggested another possibility. He thought that by concentrating on Hitler's statements and speculating about the existence or absence of personal orders by Hitler, there is a danger of underplaying the changing circumstances which may have affected Hitler's attitude to such a key issue. Hitler *may* have been unsure about what to do with the Jews. By 1941–2, with millions of Jews suddenly under his control, extermination became a feasible option. It was the changing situation in the East which may have prompted Hitler into action. Whether or not the planning was long-term, or completely improvised, Hitler was still 'responsible' for what happened.

THE 'HITLER MYTH'

Some recent studies of the Nazi period have sought to combine an analysis of Hitler the man with a reasoned investigation into his political role in Germany. Ian Kershaw made an attempt to separate the myth and reality of Hitler's career in *The Hitler Myth*, published in 1987. Kershaw studied the development and decline of the 'Hitler Myth' as it was deliberately used to cultivate support for the regime and its aims. He highlighted the way in which Hitler was presented as the personification of the nation, aloof from sectional concerns; and how his charismatic potential was exploited to win support for the Nazis. As Bullock also recognised, although this approach brought many advantages to the Nazis, the converse was that Hitler increasingly came to feel the need to live up to his image. It was then that self-deception set in and the flaws were increasingly evident.

Kershaw's was an intelligent attempt to put Hitler the man into a broader context. Historians of the Third Reich will continue to focus both on the structures and the personalities, and the better ones will probably attempt to relate the two. It is unlikely that many new facts about Hitler's career will emerge, but interest in him will continue, and interpretations of his significance will, too. That is as it should be, as each historian brings his or her own background, research, prejudices and absorption of other interpretations, to bear on the study of such an enigma as Hitler – a man who in Bullock's phrase, managed to combine paranoia and charisma. The remarkable combination ultimately failed Hitler. The man who acted as if Europe, with Germany at its centre, could control the world, hastened the process by which both German and European predominance on the international stage was destroyed. He was both Germany's fate and misfortune, but not Germany's alone.

Points to consider

1) **What difficulties does the historian face in trying to write a life of Hitler?**
2) **Assess the strengths and weaknesses of any historical study of Hitler with which you are familiar.**
3) **What are meant by the terms 'structuralist' and 'intentionalist' when applied to Hitler and Nazi Germany? Are such labels useful?**
4) **Compare and contrast the ways in which any two historians have dealt with the same episode or theme in Hitler's career.**

BIBLIOGRAPHY

Two accessible general histories of Germany in this period are:

W. Carr, *A History of Germany, 1815–1985*, (Edward Arnold, 4th ed., 1992)
G. Layton, *Germany: The Third Reich 1933–1945*, (Hodder and Stoughton, 1992)

There are many books which are informative about Hitler. The following are just a few that I have found helpful:

A. Bullock, *Hitler: A Study in Tyranny*, (Penguin, 1962)
A. Bullock, *Hitler and Stalin: Parallel Lives*, (HarperCollins, 1991)
W. Carr, *Hitler: A Study in Personality and Politics*, (Edward Arnold, 1978)
J. Hiden and J. Farquharson, *Explaining Hitler's Germany*, (2nd ed., Batsford, 1989)
K. Hildebrand, *The Third Reich*, (George Allen and Unwin, 1984)
A. Hitler, *Hitler's Table Talk*, (Weidenfeld and Nicholson, 1953)
I. Kershaw, *The Nazi Dictatorship: Problems and Perspectives*, (2nd ed., Edward Arnold, 1989)
W. Maser, *Hitler*, (Allen Lane, 1973)
E. M. Robertson, *Hitler's Pre-War Policy and Military Plans 1933–1939*, (Longman, 1963)
P. Schramm, *Hitler: The Man and the Military Leader*, (Allen Lane, 1972)
J. Stern, *Hitler, the Führer and the People*, (Fontana, 1975)
A. J. P. Taylor, *The Origins of the Second World War*, (Hamish Hamilton, 1961)
R. Waite, *The Psychopathic God: Adolf Hitler*, (Basic Books, 1977)

INDEX